W9-DFA-313

TALK OF THE BLOCK
Teacher's Guide

Ann Haffner
ESL/Literacy Educator

New Readers Press

Funded by
Massachusetts Department of Education,
Young Adults with Learning Disabilities Project

Reviewers
Mary Davilas, Beverly Gonsalves: *Brockton Adult Learning Center, Brockton, MA*
Sarah Emilio: *Community Action of Haverhill, Haverhill, MA*
Laura Brooks, Theresa Brown, Susan Nylen Quesada: *Community Learning Center, Cambridge, MA*
Marcia Chaffee, Lee Haller, Jennifer Wellman: *International Institute of Boston, Boston, MA*
Charissa Ahlstrom: *Jamaica Plain Adult Learning Program, Jamaica Plain, MA*
Anna Poor: *Jewish Vocational Services, Boston, MA*
Loreta Jordan: *Lawrence Adult Learning Center, Lawrence, MA*
Frances Laroche: *Local 26 Education Program, Boston, MA*
Charlotte Knox, Sarah Lynn, Meryl Becker: *SCALE, Somerville, MA*
Joan Fournier, Susan Wladis: *Taunton Adult Literacy Center/Bristol Community College, Fall River, MA*
Blanca Folkman, Kelley Snowden, Linda Threadgill, Holly Gannon: *Literacy Volunteers of America/East Texas Literacy Council, Longview, TX*
Bonnie Odiorne, Dave Rado, Anne Smith, Susan Weretelnik: *Literacy Volunteers of America, Waterbury, CT*

Talk of the Block Teacher's Guide
ISBN 1-56420-456-1

Printed in the United States of America
9 8 7 6 5 4 3 2 1

All proceeds from the sale of New Readers Press materials support literacy programs in the United States and worldwide.

Acquisitions Editor: Paula L. Schlusberg
Content Editor: Terrie Lipke
Production Manager: Andrea Woodbury
Designer: Andrea Woodbury
Production Specialist: Jeffrey R. Smith
Cover Design: Kimbrly Koennecke

Contents

Talk of the Block comprises two sets of four books each. One set focuses on words with short-vowel sounds, consonant digraphs, and consonant blends. The other set focuses on words with long-vowel sounds and also features vowel digraphs. Key sight words are integrated throughout.

Each *Talk of the Block* book centers on one of four key themes—family, home, shopping, and health. Every lesson begins with a story that introduces a real-life issue for adult learners such as parents helping children succeed in school, tenants dealing with a landlord, consumers shopping at a supermarket, or patients visiting a health clinic. The stories feature four central characters that live and work on an urban street block.

Talk of the Block books can be used in any order. Stories include descriptive narratives, dialogues, phone conversations, written letters, and problem-posing anecdotes. Lines in stories are numbered to make it easy to direct learners to particular words or sentences.

Following is one approach for sequencing activities to introduce and practice a *Talk of the Block* story. In a beginning-level classroom, one story may require two or more class periods for basic instruction. This example assumes that the class meets for a $2\frac{1}{2}$-hour period each week, with a 15-minute break. (For detailed information about activities that are listed, refer to the appropriate sections in Strategies & Suggestions.)

Class Session One

1. Letters and sounds practice (5 min.)

2. Word-analysis instruction and practice (30 min.)
   - Review and/or introduce sounds and/or letter patterns that appear in the story.
   - Introduce phonetically regular vocabulary words that appear in the story.
   - Practice reading vocabulary words.
   - Use other appropriate word-analysis activities (worksheets, games, etc.) to reinforce target sounds, letter patterns, and vocabulary words.

3. Sight-word instruction and practice (10 min.)
   - Review and/or introduce high-frequency words and sight words (words that are not phonetically regular) that appear in or relate to the story.
   - Practice reading high-frequency and sight words using flash cards or other activities.

4. Story reading (30 min.)
   - Prereading preparation: brainstorm, preview title, illustration, and text.
   - Reading: whole class reads the story and then discusses it.

5. Reading comprehension activities (30 min.)

6. Life-skill exercise *OR* grammar and language-structure activities (30 min.)

Class Session Two

1. Letters and sounds practice (5 min.)

2. Word-analysis instruction and practice (30 min.)
   - Review sounds and/or letter patterns that appear in the story.
   - Review phonetically regular vocabulary words that appear in the story.
   - Practice reading and spelling vocabulary words.
   - Use other appropriate word-analysis activities (worksheets, games, etc.) to reinforce target sounds, letter patterns, and vocabulary words.

3. Sight-word instruction and practice (10 min.)
   - Review high-frequency words and sight words (words that are not phonetically regular) that appear in or relate to the story.
   - Practice reading and spelling high-frequency and sight words using flash cards or other activities.

4. Story reading (30 min.)
   - Review story orally.
   - Reading: read the story again as a whole class, in partners, or individually.

5. Continued reading comprehension activities (30 min.)

6. Continued life-skill exercise *OR* grammar and language-structure activities (30 min.).

Word Analysis

Overview

Good readers read quickly, automatically recognizing letters and whole words, maintaining a pace that allows them to understand the text with relative ease. Adults learning to read and write in English need a lot of practice to develop fluency in word recognition. Explicit and systematic instruction in word-analysis skills can help adult learners to easily and automatically process text by recognizing the sounds of letters and letter combinations. The *Talk of the Block* stories were written to emphasize certain word-analysis skills and give learners opportunities to practice them.

Use stories in the short-vowel books to help learners practice reading and recognizing these types of words:

- words with short-vowel sounds
- words with short-vowel sounds that follow the consonant-vowel-consonant (CVC) pattern
- words that begin or end with the consonant digraphs *ch, ck, sh, th,* or *wh*
- words that begin or end with consonant blends
- words that have two closed syllables, have *r*-controlled vowels, or end in *-all*

Use stories in the long-vowel books to help learners practice reading and recognizing these types of words:

- words with long-vowel sounds
- words with the vowel digraphs *ai, ay, ea, ee,* or *oa*
- words with long-vowel sounds that follow the final *e* rule
- words with short-vowel sounds, CVC words, words with consonant digraphs or blends
- words that have two or three closed syllables or end in *-er, -ing, -ight, -ign,* or *-all*

The lesson notes include lists of target vocabulary words for each story. The target vocabulary words are sorted into the above categories.

Spend approximately 30 minutes at the beginning of each class teaching and practicing word analysis. Introducing and practicing story vocabulary through word analysis will prepare learners to read the story.

Teaching Suggestions

Begin by choosing several phonetically regular target vocabulary words from the story you plan to read. You may choose to focus on a particular sound or letter pattern, e.g., /th/ or CVC. Following are some strategies you can use to teach word-analysis skills with a *Talk of the Block* story:

- Present target vocabulary words one at a time to the class by writing them on the board, handing out a worksheet, or showing flash cards. Demonstrate how to read each word by sounding out the letters. For example, with *tub,* first model the individual sounds: /t/-/uh/-/b/. Then read the word *tub,* bringing the individual sounds together.

- Have learners practice reading and pronouncing target vocabulary. Ask the whole class to read words from the list chorally, then intermittently call on an individual to read a single word. Learners can also work in pairs or in small groups to practice reading the words.

- Have learners make their own flash cards for target vocabulary. Have them use one side of the cards to highlight or underline focus skills (e.g., short vowels, digraphs, or letter patterns) within words. Have learners alphabetize their flash cards. (Note: If learners also make flash cards for sight words, have them use a different color ink or card to denote vocabulary for word-analysis instruction.)

- Ask learners to create personal dictionaries using spiral notebooks. Allotting a few pages for each letter, have learners label the top of each page with the letters *A–Z.* Each time you begin a new story, have learners write the target vocabulary in their notebooks. Ask them to add their own definitions by writing sentences using the words or by drawing pictures to illustrate the words. Encourage learners to be creative. For example, for the word *family,* a learner could list the names of family members or paste a family photo on the page. (Note: If learners write sight words in this notebook, have them use a different color to distinguish sight words from phonetically regular words. This will help them to apply appropriate reading strategies.)

- Choose target vocabulary words that are easily illustrated and make two sets of flash cards: one set with words and one set with pictures. Learners can use the flash cards to do the following activities:

  - Read each word and find the matching picture.
  - Look at a picture, find the matching word, and read or write it.
  - Sort cards by letter patterns or letters (beginning or ending sounds, vowel sounds, etc.).
  - Play card games, such as Concentration or Go Fish.

- Ask learners to label pictures in the *Talk of the Block* story with appropriate vocabulary words.

- Have learners locate target vocabulary words in the story. Ask them to underline, circle, or highlight the words.

- Have learners find words in the story that contain a target sound (represented by a letter or letter combination) or letter pattern (e.g., the *sh* consonant digraph or the CVC letter pattern). Learners can work alone, in pairs, or in small groups.

- Reinforce reading fluency by introducing relevant word families. For example, after learners have practiced decoding the target vocabulary words *tub, bath,* and *fix,* introduce and practice other words in those word families (e.g., *tub: rub, sub; bath: math, path;* and *fix: mix, six*).

- Use minimal pairs for more practice. For example, after learners have practiced decoding the target vocabulary words *tub, bath,* and *fix,* introduce and practice words that have a minimal difference (e.g., *tub: tab, bath: bat,* and *fix: fox*). Add these new words when working with word and picture flash cards.

- When learners come to a word that they do not know, have them underline each consonant and make its sound. Then have them blend the sounds of all the consonants together to make a word. Ask if the word they sound out fits in the context of the sentence (e.g., *We have to pay for r-p-rs: repairs.*).

- Give learners cloze exercises to practice vocabulary words. Ask learners to say or write the missing word in sentence cloze exercises (e.g., *Bob had a bath in the ____.*) to test comprehension. Ask them to supply the missing letter(s) in word cloze exercises (e.g., *t __ b*).

- Create flash cards by writing a target word on one side (e.g., *sleep*) and writing the same word—missing key letters—on the opposite side (e.g., *sl __ __ p*). Have learners supply the missing letters. Use the flash cards for spelling and dictation work to focus on a specific phonetic element.

- Create worksheets or exercises by listing target words and other words, such as word-family words and/or minimal pairs. Read random words aloud and ask learners to circle the words they hear. This is a listening reinforcement exercise that supports word-analysis skills. Grouping similar words increases the challenge.

- Give learners weekly spelling tests using target vocabulary to reinforce word-analysis skills. First, model spelling strategies by 1) saying a word aloud, 2) breaking the word into sounds (phonemes), and 3) identifying the letters associated with the sounds. Guide learners through this procedure, modeling it until they are able to do it on their own. On tests, ask learners to distinguish between phonetically regular words and sight words. They may, for example, print phonetically regular words and write sight words in cursive. Or they can make two columns on their papers and write phonetically regular words in one column and sight words in the other.

Sight Words & High-Frequency Words

Overview

The following list contains words that appear frequently throughout *Talk of the Block*. The list includes some of the most common words in written English. Studying these words will help learners not only with *Talk of the Block*, but with overall reading fluency and comprehension as well.

This list includes both phonetically regular and irregular words. Because learners cannot use phonics rules to decode irregular words, they must learn to recognize them by sight, as whole words. The sight words in this list are marked with an asterisk (*).

The words without an asterisk follow regular phonics rules. Teach learners to sound them out while reading (see Word Analysis). Or introduce them with other words on this list as common vocabulary words learners need to know.

75 Common Sight Words* & High-Frequency Words in *Talk of the Block*		
a*	has*	some*
about	have*	talk*
am	he	tell
and	help	that
are*	her	the*
ask	his*	then
at	home	there*
be	how	they*
but	I	think
call	in	this*
can	is*	to*
can't	it	too
come*	let's	up
day	look	want*
did	lot	was*
do*	more	we
does*	my	what*
don't	need	when
for	not	where*
from	of*	who*
get	on	will
go	put*	with
good	says*	work*
got	see	you*
had	she	your*
* Sight words (phonetically irregular words that must be learned by sight or memorized)		

Some two-letter words on this list have short-vowel sounds. Since they are very common and do not follow the CVC letter pattern, which is the focus of the short-vowel books, they are listed with other high-frequency words.

Teaching Suggestions

Sight words must be introduced, reviewed, and practiced regularly in adult reading programs. Use the list of words provided here, choose a list from another source, or create your own list of sight words from particular *Talk of the Block* stories or other sources.

Following are some strategies you can use to introduce sight words to learners:

- Write the word on a flash card or in large letters on the board. Say the word aloud, then spell it, then say it again. For example, say, *"Where, W-H-E-R-E, where."* For emphasis, underline the word with your finger as you say it the final time.

- Make sight-word flash cards using index cards. Use colored index cards or colored ink to distinguish sight words from phonetically regular vocabulary words.

- Point out clues in a word that can help learners to remember it. For example, the sight words *where* and *there* include the word *here*. This reference to place may help learners remember that the words have related meanings.

- Use tactile methods to aid memorization by asking learners to trace the word on a flash card or on the board. Learners can also use a finger to write the word on the desk or table. Tracing or writing a word while saying it aloud may help learners to associate the sound of the word with the written word.

- Use gross motor skills to aid memorization by having learners air-write the word. Tell learners to extend an arm and point with one or two fingers. Then they visualize the word in big letters and say it aloud. Next, while they spell the word, learners write the word in the air with their fingers.

- Some learners may respond better to auditory cues, so try using chanting to aid memorization. Ask learners to help make up rhythmic chants to practice spelling and saying words, e.g., *"W-H . . . E-R-E, Where? Where?"*

- Learners may find it easer to remember meanings if you teach some sight words in related groups, e.g., *there* and *where,* or *could, would,* and *should.*

Use the following methods to practice and reinforce sight words:

- Teach sight words systematically. Choose two or three new words for learners to study each week. Keep a list of all sight words taught, and occasionally review them throughout the year.

- Have learners make and keep their own set of sight-word flash cards. They should use color to distinguish sight words from regular vocabulary flash cards.

- Have learners add sight words to their personal dictionaries. Encourage them to add their own definitions by writing sentences using the words or by drawing pictures to illustrate the words. (Note: Have learners use a different color to distinguish phonetically regular words from sight words. This will help them to apply appropriate reading strategies.)

- Create a word wall in the classroom. Write sight words on the word wall as they are learned.

- Have learners locate sight words in the story. Ask them to underline, circle, or highlight the words.

- Give learners cloze exercises to practice sight words. Ask learners to say or write the missing word in sentence cloze exercises (e.g., *Bob had a bath in _____ tub.*) to test comprehension. Ask them to supply the missing letter(s) in word cloze exercises (e.g., *t __ e*) to practice spelling.

- Include sight words in weekly spelling tests. Make sure learners have practiced different strategies for remembering sight words before you test them. Test sight words separately from phonetically regular words. Or, as learners progress, have them distinguish between phonetically regular words and sight words by printing phonetically regular words and writing sight words in cursive. Or they can make two columns on their papers and write phonetically regular words in one column and sight words in the other.

Vocabulary

Overview

The *Talk of the Block* stories contain simple, yet relevant, vocabulary. The Lesson Notes for each story include a list of target vocabulary words. The words appear in these three categories:

1. Word analysis: Phonetically regular words that can be used to teach word-analysis skills

2. Sight words & high-frequency words: Phonetically irregular words that must be learned by sight and common phonetically regular words that appear frequently in *Talk of the Block*

3. Challenge words & phrases: More challenging vocabulary words (which may or may not be phonetically regular) and common phrases that can be learned in the context of the story

Teaching Suggestions

- Use the target vocabulary list to choose a list of vocabulary words for each story. Choose an assortment of words from each category.

- Introduce vocabulary words to learners before they begin to tackle a story. Make sure they understand the words they need to read the story.

- Refer to the previous sections (Word Analysis and Sight Words & High-Frequency Words) for teaching ideas.

- Continually recycle and review vocabulary words. Learners can keep track of words they have studied by adding them to either their flash cards or their personal dictionaries.

- Teach learners to use context to help them understand vocabulary words. Point out a word in the story and have learners visualize what is happening and predict what the word might mean. Ask them to substitute other words for the vocabulary word to help them understand or to show they understand the word's meaning.

Following are some general suggestions for teaching vocabulary:

- Create flash cards for target vocabulary words in each story. Use card or ink color to give learners clues about the words. For instance, use black ink for phonetically regular words that learners can sound out, and use red ink for sight words that need to be memorized. Or use colored cards to help teach grammar and parts of speech, e.g., yellow cards for nouns, orange cards for days of week/subject pronouns/proper nouns, green cards for verbs, blue cards for describing words (adjectives, possessive pronouns, etc.), and white cards for articles, etc.

- After introducing vocabulary flash cards for a story, display them in the classroom and refer to them while working on the story. Pocket charts can be used to display flash cards as well as sentence strips.

- Play card games with vocabulary flash cards:
    - Have learners sort cards by letter patterns or sounds (beginning sound, ending sound, vowel sound, etc.).
    - Have learners sort sight words from phonetically regular words.
    - Have learners sort words by category (e.g., foods, places, actions, etc.).

- Choose target vocabulary words that are easily illustrated and make two sets of flash cards: one set with words and one set with pictures. Where possible, use real-life representations (realia) or photos to illustrate words (e.g., a copy of a voided check for *check*, a family photo for *family*, etc.). Learners can use the flash cards to do the following activities:

  - Read each word and find the matching picture.
  - Look at a picture, find the matching word, and read or write it.
  - Sort cards by letter patterns or letters (beginning or ending sounds, vowel sounds, etc.).

- Make word search puzzles using vocabulary words from a story. Hand them out on worksheets or display them on an overhead.

- Use oral and written cloze exercises to reinforce word meanings. If vocabulary words are displayed in the room, learners can easily refer to them. Use sentences from the stories for cloze exercises (e.g., *Bob has a _____ in the tub.*). Ask learners to say or write the missing vocabulary word.

- Play "What's in the Bag?" to practice vocabulary meanings. Fill up a few bags with pictures and/or realia to represent vocabulary words. In small groups, have learners work together to create a list of what is in the bag. Learners can check their spelling using vocabulary lists in the room, their personal dictionaries, or flash cards.

- Play games using target vocabulary words. Use popular game shows as models. For example, make a game like *Jeopardy!* by sorting words into categories such as spelling, parts of speech, picture match, word functions (e.g., things in a kitchen), etc. Or make a spelling game using a format like *Who Wants to Be a Millionaire.* Learners can win pennies or other small prizes by spelling words correctly. If learners need help, offer them lifelines such as asking another learner or spending 30 seconds with their personal dictionaries.

Grammar & Language Structures

Overview

Grammar in the *Talk of the Block* stories is basic enough that most learners can access the text with ease and focus on overall comprehension. Nevertheless, the *Talk of the Block* stories offer many opportunities to teach grammar skills and basic English language structures.

The lesson notes for each story include suggested grammar and language-structure topics. Following are some general suggestions for teaching grammar and language structures.

Teaching Suggestions

- Select specific sentences from the story to focus on. Make sentence strips or write sentences on the board or overhead. Have learners diagram and label the sentences. Start by labeling subjects and predicates, then move on to labeling parts of speech (nouns, verbs, adjectives, etc.).

- For beginning readers and English language learners who are not ready for complex grammar instruction, begin by pointing out phrases or chunks of sentences. Have learners practice scooping phrases or groups of words in sentences from the story. Model scooping by using your finger to scoop each phrase or part of a sentence. This helps learners to see how words and groups of words serve different functions. This also helps learners with fluency by teaching them to see words in bigger chunks instead of looking at just one word at a time. Use an overhead projector or write words on the board. Focus on a few target sentences per story. Here are some examples of scooped sentences:

  Bob can go to the clinic.

  Pam has a baby at home.

- Use colored flash cards to help teach grammar and parts of speech, e.g., yellow cards for nouns, orange cards for days of week/subject pronouns/proper nouns, green cards for verbs, blue cards for describing words (adjectives, possessive pronouns, etc.), and white cards for articles, etc.

- Use sentence strips from the story to make cloze sentences (e.g., *Bob is _____.*). Have learners choose words from vocabulary flash cards to fill in the blank. Discuss which types of words complete the sentence and why.

- Use index cards for building sentences or phrases. Put short sentences or phrases on index cards, one word per card. Have learners put the words in order. Use colored flash cards to denote parts of speech.

- Focus on one or two verbs per story. Conjugate verbs with the class. Post a verb conjugation chart in the room when working with the story.

Reading Comprehension

Overview

Reading is an active and complex process of making meaning out of written text, or symbols, on a page. Good readers do more than just decode words. They use a variety of reading comprehension strategies, such as the following, to help them derive meaning from the text. Good readers

1. read with a purpose

2. read at a pace that allows them to understand the text while recognizing letters and words

3. use a variety of strategies, depending on the text, to read efficiently—e.g., vary reading speed, predict what will happen next, preview headings and illustrations

4. interact with the text, make personal connections, and use their background knowledge

5. evaluate the text critically, ask questions, agree or disagree with the author, and identify problems in the text or things they do not understand

Effective reading instruction must also emphasize reading comprehension skills. It requires more than just word analysis and vocabulary. You need to equip new readers to be good readers. To do that, introduce learners to a variety of strategies to help them read efficiently and effectively and to construct meaning from text. When teaching reading comprehension skills, model prereading, during-reading, and postreading strategies.

Following is a list of suggestions to help develop overall reading comprehension and to model effective reading behaviors.

Teaching Suggestions

Prereading activities:

- Teach learners to preview a story before they read it. Show them how to scan the story quickly, noticing organization, content, and level of difficulty. Getting

an idea of what the story is about also activates background knowledge in the subject.

- Previewing helps learners prepare to read many kinds of text. Tell learners to look at titles and illustrations to pick up clues about the text content. Ask learners to look at an illustration or title and guess what the story is about.

- Point out text style and format. In *Talk of the Block,* stories include bold titles, numbered lines, spaces between groups of sentences (resembling paragraph transitions), and dialogue formats.

- If introducing a new book, have learners preview the entire book before they begin reading it so that they are familiar with its contents and organization. Point out the front cover, table of contents, author's name, preface and/or introduction, index, glossary, etc. Ask learners questions about the book's organization after they have previewed it. Look at some pages in detail, such as the table of contents, and ask questions, e.g., *On which page can we find the story Bob Is Sick?*

- Do a whole-class brainstorming activity to show how a title, illustration, or key word from a story can activate learners' background knowledge. Write a story title on the board or on an overhead. Ask learners to tell what they think the story might be about. Ask what they know about that subject. Make a list of learners' comments and predictions. Check the list after reading the story to see if learner predictions were correct.

- Introduce vocabulary words to learners before they begin to tackle a story. Make sure they understand the words they need to read the story.

During-reading activities:

- When reading the story for the first time, either read the story aloud or have learners read the story silently on their own. Avoid multiple starts and stops that can sometimes hinder understanding.

- After the initial reading, reread the story together as a whole class, using some of the following strategies to facilitate and support learners' comprehension.

- Encourage learners to do the following while they read:
  - visualize what is happening
  - make a personal connection to something in the story

- predict what might happen next (stop mid-story, ask learners to close their books and predict what they think will happen next)

- highlight or underline words or sentences they do not understand

• Think aloud when reading the story aloud with learners. Model how to use the strategies listed above (visualizing, connecting, predicting, identifying problem areas) when reading the story by voicing your comments or questions aloud. Thinking aloud helps involve learners directly in constructing meaning from the text. Model the think-aloud process before encouraging learners to join in. Here is an example of the think-aloud strategy:

In *Talk of the Block, Short-Vowel Stories: Health,* Bob visits Hill Street Clinic. Here are two lines from the story "At the Clinic":

Bob sits and sits and sits.
Bob sits and thinks, "I am sick of this clinic."

After reading these lines, you might think, *I know how Bob feels. Last week I went to the clinic and had to wait an hour in the waiting room before I got to see the doctor. I was so frustrated!* Say your thoughts aloud and see how learners respond.

• Discuss things learners do not understand. Use questions to facilitate their understanding. Get learners actively involved in breaking down and tackling problems so that they do understand.

• Encourage learners to reread the same story. Learners can practice reading in pairs. Conduct timed readings so that learners can see their progress.

Postreading activities:

• Use drawing and illustration exercises to reinforce story comprehension. Have learners work alone or in small groups to illustrate a portion of the story. Show the drawings to the class and have learners guess what the pictures are about. Then have learners put the pictures in order. Arrange the drawings like a comic strip. Have learners look at the drawings and retell the story in their own words or try to match parts of the story with appropriate pictures.

• Make sentence strips using sentences from the story. Draw or have learners draw pictures to illustrate the sentences. Then have learners take turns reading sentence strips and matching them with pictures.

• Use writing activities to reinforce story learning and comprehension. Encourage learners to do freewriting about a topic or theme in the story. They may want to write about a personal connection they made to the story, a question they had, or something they agreed or disagreed with.

• Have learners write a one-sentence summary of the story.

• Ask learners to write a follow-up story. If their writing skills are limited, have them dictate the story while you write it on the board or overhead.

• Use classroom discussions and listening/speaking activities to reinforce story comprehension. Have learners act out the story in role-plays.

• Have learners write their own comprehension questions about the story. Explain the 5W and H question starters: *who, what, when, where, why,* and *how.* Split the class into teams and have them use the question starters to ask each other questions about the story.

Life Skills

Overview

Connecting materials with learners' real lives and experiences has been shown to greatly enhance overall learning and learner progress. A primary goal of the *Talk of the Block* stories is to provide relevant reading materials—materials that reflect the real-life concerns, experiences, and situations of adult beginning readers.

The *Talk of the Block* stories generate focus and discussion around real-life concerns such as health insurance, tenants' rights, and advocating for oneself and one's family. Though the written language used in *Talk of the Block* is geared towards beginning readers, you can easily extend and build on story themes during classroom discussions and while working on exercises or activities. For example, practice relevant life skills that are introduced in stories, such as filling out medical forms, calling a landlord, or asking for help at the supermarket.

The lesson notes provide suggested life-skills themes and discussion topics that may be used with individual *Talk of the Block* stories. Life skills included in your own curriculum may provide additional ideas for classroom activities. Following are some general teaching suggestions for teaching life skills with adult learners.

Teaching Suggestions

- Teach life skills in thematic units, such as shopping or housing. Ask questions to determine learners' basic needs. For example, if the topic is shopping, ask questions, e.g., *Where do you shop for food? Do you know who to ask if you need help while you shop? Do you know how to ask for help?* Then have learners prioritize their needs. Use the *Talk of the Block* stories and characters to address learners' primary life-skills concerns.

- For English language learners, focus on life-skills listening/speaking activities. In these areas, take advantage of and introduce learners to a larger number of English words, not just the easily accessed phonetically regular words learners may be limited to within reading/writing activities. For instance, while reading stories about Bob going to the clinic, introduce terms learners might need to describe other illnesses or symptoms.

- Teach life skills at the end of the lesson, when learners are most likely to be tiring out from a long day at work or school. Make exercises as active and engaging as possible.

- Use real-life materials to support life-skills teaching. Collect things from the local environment: bus schedules, medical forms, calendars, food labels, doctor's appointment cards, health pamphlets, letters from landlords, apartment leases, want ads, menus, etc.

- Show learners how to use role-plays to act out situations.

- Go on field trips to the local supermarket, the pharmacy, the mall, etc.

- Recycle learned skills. For example, if check-writing skills are introduced within a shopping story, have learners also write checks to a landlord when they work on a housing story. If students learn how to write a shopping list in the shopping book, have them write a list of symptoms or questions to bring to a doctor when they work on a health story.

Lesson Notes—Short Vowels

Welcome to Hill Street

TARGET VOCABULARY

Word Analysis

Short vowels/CVC: *Jack, Pam; Hill, kids, Kim; Bob, job, lot*
Consonant digraphs: *block, Jack* (ck); *shops* (sh); *with* (th)
Consonant blends: *block* (bl); *clinic* (cl)
Other: *clinic* (2 closed syllables)

Sight Words & High-Frequency Words

a, has, is, of, on, the, this, to

Challenge Words & Phrases

a lot of, lives, Street, welcome

GRAMMAR & LANGUAGE STRUCTURES

- *this is* (in introductions)
- *to have* (verb)
- *to live* (verb)

LIFE SKILLS

- describing a street block
- describing personal addresses (e.g., *I live on . . .*)
- personal introductions

Family

Kim and the Kids

TARGET VOCABULARY

Word Analysis

Short vowels/CVC: *Ben; kids, Kim, Liz*
Consonant blends: *and* (nd)

Sight Words & High-Frequency Words

a, are, has, he, is, of, she, the, they, this

Challenge Words & Phrases

family: *daughter, family, mother, son*
numbers: *two, 10, 14*

GRAMMAR & LANGUAGE STRUCTURES

- *he, she, they* (subject pronouns)
- *'s* (with possessives)
- *this is* (in introductions)
- *to be* (verb)

LIFE SKILLS

- describing age
- family and family terms
- introductions
- numbers

Don't Miss the Bus!

TARGET VOCABULARY

Word Analysis

Short vowels/CVC: *Ben, get, let's, tells, yells; Hill, it, kids, Kim, Liz, miss; Top; bus, run*

Consonant digraphs: *backpack(s)* (ck)

Consonant blends: *and* (nd); *stop* (st)

Sight Words & High-Frequency Words

are, at, don't, go, her, his, is, on, the, they, to, your

Challenge Words & Phrases

Monday, school

bus-related: *bus stop, get the bus, miss the bus*

times: *7:15 a.m., 7:20 a.m., 7:25 a.m., 7:30 a.m.*

GRAMMAR & LANGUAGE STRUCTURES

- *don't, let's* (contractions)
- *her, his, your* (possessive pronouns)
- *it* (subject pronoun, with time)
- *let's* (imperative)
- *to have* (verb)

LIFE SKILLS

- bus travel and bus schedules
- kids and school
- morning routines
- times (*a.m.*)
- types of transportation

A Problem with Math

TARGET VOCABULARY

Word Analysis

Short vowels/CVC: *can, can't, sad; Ben, get, let's; him, Kim, sits; Mom, not*

Consonant digraphs: *math, with* (th)

Consonant blends: *help* (lp); *ask, desk* (sk)

Sight Words & High-Frequency Words

a, at, be, do, don't, for, good, he, his, home, I, is, it's, OK, says, she, talks, the, this, to, we, works, you, your

Challenge Words & Phrases

happy, maybe, problem, school, study, teacher

school: *be good at math, do math, study math, work on math*

GRAMMAR & LANGUAGE STRUCTURES

- *can* vs. *can't*
- *can't, don't, it's* (contractions)
- *don't, let's* (imperatives)
- *has to*

LIFE SKILLS

- kids and homework: making sure kids do their homework, helping kids with their homework, getting help when kids can't do their homework
- school subjects (e.g., *math*)

Kim Calls the School

TARGET VOCABULARY

Word Analysis

Short vowels/CVC: *can, mad, sad; Ben; Hill, Kim, Miss, Pitt, will; mom, Top; but*
Consonant digraphs: *back* (ck); *math, thank, with* (th)
Consonant blends: *class* (cl); *help* (lp); *and* (nd); *thank* (nk); *ask* (sk)
Other: *call/s* (-all word family)

Sight Words & High-Frequency Words

a, am, at, for, has, her, I, in, is, needs, no, not, OK, on, she, son, the, this, to, you

Challenge Words & Phrases

school, teacher
names & titles: *Ben's mom, Kim Lee, Miss Pitt*
telephone: *call, call back, hello, speak, thank you*
days: *Tuesday, Wednesday, Thursday*
times: *4:00 p.m.*

GRAMMAR & LANGUAGE STRUCTURES

- *at* (preposition of place: *at school*)
- *at* (preposition of time: *at 4:00 p.m.*)
- *but* (to signal change of direction)
- *can* (in questions)

LIFE SKILLS

- calling a school/contacting a teacher
- dealing with a secretary or telephone operator: leaving a message, calling back

Ben Gets Help with Math

TARGET VOCABULARY

Word Analysis

Short vowels/CVC: *can, can't, sad; Ben, get/s, tells; Kim, Miss, Pitt, will; not*
Consonant digraphs: *rings* (ng); *math, thinks, with* (th)
Consonant blends: *help* (lp); *ask* (sk)

Sight Words & High-Frequency Words

a, am, at, be, do, for, from, good, he, his, home, is, it, need/s, not, on, she, the, to, you

Challenge Words & Phrases

happy, teacher, tutor
days: *Tuesday, Thursday, Friday*
names & titles: *Ben's teacher, Miss Pitt*
times: *3:00 p.m., 4:00 p.m.*

GRAMMAR & LANGUAGE STRUCTURES

- *can* (in questions)
- *from* and *to* (prepositions, with times)
- *on* (preposition, with days of the week)
- *will* (to denote future)

- after-school activities and programs
- talking to a child's teacher
- tutors, getting help with schoolwork

TV or the Park?

TARGET VOCABULARY

Word Analysis

Short vowels/CVC: *can, can't; Ben, let's; kids, Kim, Liz, sit/s, will; not; run, fun*

Consonant digraphs: *kick* (ck); *with* (th)

Consonant blends: *and* (nd)

Other: *all, ball* (-*all* family); *or, park, turn* (*r*-controlled vowels)

Sight Words & High-Frequency Words

are, at, be, day, don't, go, he, home, I, in, is, it, OK, says, she, the, to, TV, want, we, work, you

Challenge Words & Phrases

not at school, not at work

days: *Sunday, weekend*

TV: *turn off the TV, watch TV*

GRAMMAR & LANGUAGE STRUCTURES

- *can* vs. *can't*
- *don't* (with negatives, e.g., *I want/don't want to*)
- *let's* (imperative)
- *not* (with negatives, e.g., *the park is fun/not fun*)

LIFE SKILLS

- day-off activities, family activities
- expressing opinions (*I want to, I don't want to*)
- local parks
- TV watching: pros and cons
- weekend vs. weekdays

Kim Gets a Rest

TARGET VOCABULARY

Word Analysis

Short vowels/CVC: *can, pans, rag; Ben, gets, let's, tell; big, fix, kids, Kim, Liz, sit; lot, Mom, mop; cups*

Consonant digraphs: *thank* (th); *wash* (sh); *wrong* (ng)

Consonant blends: *asks* (sk); *dust, rest* (st); *grin* (gr); *help* (lp); *sink, thank* (nk)

Other: *dinner* (2 closed syllables)

Sight Words & High-Frequency Words

a, am, are, at, do, for, from, go, has, he, home, I, is, it, need/s, out, says, she, the, they, to, we, what, work, you

Challenge Words & Phrases

a lot to do, thank you, tired, wrong

question: *What is wrong?*

household: *cups, dust, mop, pans, rag, sink, wash*

meals: *fix dinner, go out for dinner*

GRAMMAR & LANGUAGE STRUCTURES

- *can*
- *has to*
- *I* (in personal descriptions, e.g., *I am tired.*)
- *needs to*
- *what* questions

LIFE SKILLS

- asking kids to help/delegating responsibilities
- chores and household responsibilities
- housecleaning activities

Home

A New Apartment

TARGET VOCABULARY

Word Analysis

Short vowels/CVC: *can, Jack, Pam; bedroom, tells; will; Bob, box, not*

Consonant digraphs: *bathroom, that, with* (th); *Jack, unpack* (ck)

Consonant blends: *and* (nd); *fast, stop* (st); *help* (lp)

Other: *all* (-*all* family); *unpack, kitchen* (2 closed syllables)

Sight Words & High-Frequency Words

a, at, day, has, in, it, new, OK, on, put, says, so, the, they, this, time, we, work

Challenge Words & Phrases

apartment, new, not so fast, one . . . at a time

housing: *apartment, bathroom, bedroom, kitchen, living room, room(s)*

numbers: *one, four*

GRAMMAR & LANGUAGE STRUCTURES

- *put* (in directions, e.g., *put this . . . , put that . . .*)
- *it* (subject pronoun)
- *this* vs. *that*

LIFE SKILLS

- getting help from friends
- housing vocabulary
- moving into a new apartment

Jack's Apartment

TARGET VOCABULARY

Word Analysis

Short vowels/CVC: *fan, pans; bed; pots; rug, tub*

Consonant digraphs: *bathroom* (th); *Jack* (ck)

Consonant blends: *and* (nd); *lamp* (mp); *next* (xt); *sink* (nk)

Sight Words & High-Frequency Words

a, an, are, has, his, in, is, the, there, this, to

Challenge Words & Phrases

happy

housing: *apartment, bathroom, bedroom, kitchen, living room*

GRAMMAR & LANGUAGE STRUCTURES

- *in, next to, under* (prepositions of place)
- *there is/there are*

LIFE SKILLS

- describing your apartment/house
- housing vocabulary
- locating household items (e.g., *Where is the _____?*)

Neighbors

TARGET VOCABULARY

Word Analysis

Short vowels/CVC: *Pam; Hill*

Consonant digraphs: *Jack* (ck)

Consonant blends: *friends* (nd); *next* (xt)

Sight Words & High-Frequency Words

an, are, has, he, in, is, on, she, they, to

Challenge Words & Phrases

addresses: *address, apartment, street*

neighbors, friends, live/s, next to

numbers: *3, 5, 24*

GRAMMAR & LANGUAGE STRUCTURES

- **addresses:** house numbers, street names, apartment numbers
- *in, next to, on* (prepositions of place)
- *'s* (with possessives, e.g., *Jack's, Pam's*)

LIFE SKILLS

- housing *(apartment, duplex, house, etc.)*
- neighbors
- numbers
- stating your address

A Crack in the Tub

TARGET VOCABULARY

Word Analysis

Short vowels/CVC: *can; gets, tell, wet; fix, will; Gus, rug, tub*

Consonant digraphs: *checks, crack, Jack* (ck); *bath, with* (th)

Consonant blends: *crack* (cr); *drips* (dr); *and* (nd); *fast* (st)

Sight Words & High-Frequency Words

a, at, has, in, is, says, the, this, to, up

Challenge Words & Phrases

every morning, floor, landlord, problem, this morning

expression: *Oh no!*

times: *6:00 a.m., 6:05 a.m.*

GRAMMAR & LANGUAGE STRUCTURES

- *every* and *this* (as qualifying adjectives, e.g., *every/this morning*)

- *to be* (verb, in descriptions, e.g., *rug is wet, floor is wet*)
- *will* (to denote future)

LIFE SKILLS

- landlord's responsibilities
- morning/daily routines
- problems in the apartment
- time

Call the Landlord

TARGET VOCABULARY

Word Analysis

Short Vowels/CVC: *can; tell, yes; fix, will; not; Gus, tub*
Consonant digraphs: *crack, Jack* (ck); *ring* (ng); *phone* (ph); *with* (th); *when* (wh)
Consonant blends: *crack* (cr); *drips* (dr); *and* (nd); *fast* (st)
Other: *call* (-*all* family)

Sight Words & High-Frequency Words

a, has, have, he, his, I, in, is, it, OK, on, or, the, this, to, what, you

Challenge Words & Phrases

answers, Apartment 3, has a problem, hello, landlord, plumber
days: *Thursday, Friday, today*

GRAMMAR & LANGUAGE STRUCTURES

- *can*
- *to have* (verb)
- *what* and *when* questions
- *will* (to denote future)

LIFE SKILLS

- calling/speaking to a landlord
- describing problems in the apartment/house
- people who repair things (plumber, etc.)
- telephone routines/introductions

The Trash Truck

TARGET VOCABULARY

Word Analysis

Short vowels/CVC: *bags, cans; bed, get/s, tells, yells; bin, kids, Kim; run*
Consonant digraphs: *bang* (ng); *crash, trash* (sh); *quick, truck* (ck); *thud* (th)
Consonant blends: crash (cr); *glass* (gl); *grab/s* (gr); *help* (lp); *end* (nd); *fast, stop/s, street* (st); *trash, truck* (tr); *next* (xt)

Sight Words & High-Frequency Words

at, her, in, is, it, need, of, on, put, she, that, the, they, this, to, up, your

Challenge Words & Phrases

next to, street
trash terms: *bags, bin, cans, glass, trash*
days & times: *Friday, 6:30 a.m.*

GRAMMAR & LANGUAGE STRUCTURES

- *at the end of, in, next to* (prepositions of place, e.g., *at the end of the street, in bed, next to Kim*)
- *get/s up*
- *get* and *put* (in directions, e.g., *get the glass . . . , put the cans . . .*)
- *this* vs. *that*

LIFE SKILLS

- getting kids to help
- morning routines
- trash pickup and recycling

Time to Pay Rent

TARGET VOCABULARY

Word Analysis

Short vowels/CVC: *Pam; let's; will; Gus*

Consonant digraphs: *check(s), Jack* (ck)

Consonant blends: *and* (nd); *rent* (nt)

Other: *calls* (-all family), *forget* (2 closed syllables)

Sight Words & High-Frequency Words

a, day, don't, for, give/s, has, he, his, I, is, it, it's, month, OK, of, pay/s, says, she, the, time, to, writes

Challenge Words & Phrases

apartment, landlord

days: *day, today, month, every month*

rent: *pay(s) rent, write a check, give a check to the landlord*

GRAMMAR & LANGUAGE STRUCTURES

- *don't, it's, let's* (contractions)
- *every* (as a qualifying adjective, e.g., *every month*)
- *has to*

LIFE SKILLS

- money and check writing
- paying rent
- tenant's responsibilities

Shopping

Shopping Day

TARGET VOCABULARY

Word Analysis

Short vowels/CVC: *can, Pam, pan; get, sells; will; Bob's, not*

Consonant digraphs: *fish, fresh, shop/s* (sh); *things* (th)

Consonant blends: *dress* (dr); *fresh* (fr)

Other: *all, mall* (-all family)

Sight Words & High-Frequency Words

a, at, day, for, go, has, her, home, is, it, on, she, the, this, to, work

Challenge Words & Phrases

food, shopping day, store

days: *Saturday, day off*

stores: *Home Store, mall, supermarket, Save-a-Lot, Hill Street Fish Market*

GRAMMAR & LANGUAGE STRUCTURES

- *at, in, to* (prepositions, e.g., *at Home Store, in the mall, to the supermarket*
- *can*
- *has to*

LIFE SKILLS

- day-off activities
- places to shop
- shopping lists

A Pan for Pam

TARGET VOCABULARY

Word Analysis

Short vowels/CVC: *Pam, pan/s, that; get/s, sells; will; lot, not, pots; but*

Consonant digraphs: *much* (ch); *shops* (sh); *things, thinks, thrift* (th)

Consonant blends: *thrift* (ft); *and, secondhand* (nd); *thinks* (nk); *cost/s, stops* (st); *next* (xt)

Sight Words & High-Frequency Words

a, are, at, do, for, good, has, is, it, money, sees, she, that, the, this, to, too

Challenge Words & Phrases

a lot, Home Store, secondhand store, thrift, Thrifty Shop

prices: *cost a lot, (not) too much money, $5.00, $25.00*

GRAMMAR & LANGUAGE STRUCTURES

- *at, next to* (prepositions of place, e.g., *at/next to Home Store*)
- *but* (to signal change of direction)
- *has to*
- *not* (as a quantifier, e.g., *not too much, not a lot*)

LIFE SKILLS

- comparing prices
- kitchen items
- shopping strategies
- thrift shops, buying secondhand

A New Dress

TARGET VOCABULARY

Word Analysis

Short vowels/CVC: *bag, can, can't, Pam; get/s; fit, will; but*

Consonant digraphs: *back, black* (ck); *bring/s* (ng)

Consonant blends: *belt* (lt); *black* (bl); *dress* (dr); *thinks* (nk)

Other: *mall* (-all family)

Sight Words & High-Frequency Words

a, at, for, good, has, in, it, is, OK, puts, says, sees, she, the, this, to, today, was, you

Challenge Words & Phrases

cashier, new dress, pays, store

clothing: *black, belt, fit*

prices: *$10.00, $40.00, $50.00*

shopping: *$10.00 off, (can't) bring it back*

GRAMMAR & LANGUAGE STRUCTURES

- *bring back*
- *can* vs. *can't*
- *to be* (in descriptions, e.g., *it is black, it is $10 off*)
- *is* vs. *was*

LIFE SKILLS

- clothing items, colors, sizes, styles, etc.
- return policies
- sales, types of sales, discounts
- talking to a cashier

A Rip in the Dress

TARGET VOCABULARY

Word Analysis

Short vowels/CVC: *bag, can, can't, Pam; did, rip; got, not; bus, but*

Consonant digraphs: *back* (ck); *thinks, with* (th)

Consonant blends: *bring* (br); *dress* (dr); *thinks* (nk); *problem* (pr); *just, stop* (st); *next* (xt)

Other: *mall, small* (-all family)

Sight Words & High-Frequency Words

a, at, has, her, in, is, it, looks, of, says, sees, she, the, was, what, you

Challenge Words & Phrases

bus stop, cashier, new dress, problem, said, store

expression: *Oh no!*

shopping: *can't bring it back, cashier, rip in the dress, $10.00 off*

GRAMMAR & LANGUAGE STRUCTURES

- *at, in, next to, with* (prepositions, e.g., *at the bus stop, in the bag, next to the mall, with the dress*)
- *just* (to describe time, e.g., *Pam just got a new dress.*)
- present tense vs. past tense

LIFE SKILLS

- buying sale items
- store return policies
- talking to store personnel/customer service

The Shopping List

TARGET VOCABULARY

Word Analysis

Short vowels/CVC: *jam, Pam; eggs, get/s; lot*

Consonant digraphs: *shop/s* (sh); *when* (wh)

Consonant blends: *milk* (lk); *helps* (lp); *and* (nd); *list* (st)

Other: *basket* (2 closed syllables)

Sight Words & High-Frequency Words

a, at, for, has, her, in, is, it, of, on, she, the, to, what

Challenge Words & Phrases

walks

shopping: *food, Save-a-Lot, shopping list, store, supermarket, writes a list*

GRAMMAR & LANGUAGE STRUCTURES

- *has to*
- commas with lists of items in sentences
- numbered lists

LIFE SKILLS

- food items
- making shopping lists
- places to shop for food (supermarket, outdoor markets, corner stores, etc.)

At the Checkout

TARGET VOCABULARY

Word Analysis

Short vowels/CVC: *jam, Pam; eggs, get, tells; bill, will*

Consonant digraphs: *checkout, much* (ch); *cash* (sh)

Consonant blends: *milk* (lk); *asks* (sk); *costs, stops* (st)

Other: *basket* (2 closed syllables)

Sight Words & High-Frequency Words

a, are, at, has, her, how, is, of, she, the, to, what

Challenge Words & Phrases

cashier, change, checkout, food, gives, Save-a-Lot, supermarket

prices: *$1.25, $2.60, $3.25, $7.10, $10.00*

GRAMMAR & LANGUAGE STRUCTURES

- *how much is* vs. *how much are*
- *how much* questions
- *to be* (verb)

LIFE SKILLS

- asking the price of an item
- prices and numbers
- shopping math: totaling a bill, figuring and adding tax, getting and making change
- supermarkets (e.g., types of checkout lines)

Hill Street Fish Market

TARGET VOCABULARY

Word Analysis

Short vowels/CVC: *can, Pam, ran; get/s, sells; did, will; Bob, not, but, runs*

Consonant digraphs: *locks* (ck); *fish, fresh, rush* (sh)

Consonant blends: *fresh* (fr); *and* (nd); *asks* (sk); *smells* (sm)

Sight Words & High-Frequency Words

a, are, at, from, has, he, I, in, is, on, says, she, some, the, there, to, today, up, we

Challenge Words & Phrases

fresh fish, happy, Hill Street Fish Market, like

days: *Saturday, Sunday, Monday*

stores: *close, closed, locks up, open*

times: *8:00 a.m., 9:00 a.m., 5:00 p.m., 5:05 p.m.*

GRAMMAR & LANGUAGE STRUCTURES

- *but* (to signal change of direction)
- *from* and *to* (prepositions, with time)
- *like* (in descriptions, similes)
- *run/ran, get/did not get* (past tense)

LIFE SKILLS

- days of the week
- fresh food markets, specialty markets, outdoor markets, farmers' markets, etc.
- store hours and schedules
- times

Health

Call the Clinic

TARGET VOCABULARY

Word Analysis

Short vowels/CVC: *bad, can, Pam; Ben, legs, yes; Hill, him, Kim; son*

Consonant digraphs: *chest* (ch); *neck, sick* (ck); *bring* (ng); *rash* (sh); *thank* (th); *what* (wh)

Consonant blends: *bring* (br); *clinic* (cl); *help* (lp); *and, hands* (nd); *thank* (nk); *chest* (st)

Other: *call* (-*all* family); *clinic, doctor, matter* (2 closed syllables)

Sight Words & High-Frequency Words

a, at, come, has, he, her, his, I, is, it, my, OK, on, see, the, this, to, today, was, we, what, what's, you

Challenge Words & Phrases

doctor, hello, Hill Street Clinic, Kim Lee, name

body parts: *chest, hands, legs, neck*

days: *Monday, Tuesday, Wednesday*

doctor appointment questions: *What's the matter? May I help you? Can you bring him in today at 1:00 p.m.?*

time: *1:00 p.m.*

GRAMMAR & LANGUAGE STRUCTURES

- *is* vs. *was* (present vs. past)
- *may* and *can* questions
- *my* (possessive pronoun, e.g., *my son, my name*)
- *what's* (contraction)

LIFE SKILLS

- days of the week
- describing illness, types of symptoms/illnesses (*rash, sore throat, cough,* etc.)
- making an appointment on the telephone
- parts of the body

Bob Is Sick

TARGET VOCABULARY

Word Analysis

Short vowels/CVC: *can, can't; bed, get, well; will; Bob, boss*

Consonant digraphs: *sick* (ck); *thank* (th)

Consonant blends: *clinic* (cl); *help* (lp); *and* (nd); *thank* (nk)

Other: *calls* (*-all* family); *clinic* (2 closed syllables)

Sight Words & High-Frequency Words

am, at, come, go, he, I, in, is, OK, says, the, to, today, this, want, we, work, you

Challenge Words & Phrases

get well, go/come to work, in bed, Hill Street Clinic

GRAMMAR & LANGUAGE STRUCTURES

- *can* vs. *can't*
- *to be* (in descriptions, e.g., *I am sick, Bob is sick*)
- *will* (to denote future)

LIFE SKILLS

- calling a clinic or doctor's office
- calling the boss when you are sick
- describing illness
- getting help when you are sick (going to a clinic, hospital, doctor, etc.)

At the Clinic

TARGET VOCABULARY

Word Analysis

Short vowels/CVC: *can, Pam; get, tells, well; big, Finn, Hill, sit/s; Bob*

Consonant digraphs: *sick* (ck); *thinks, then, with* (th)

Consonant blends: *clinic* (cl); *help/s* (lp); *and, stands* (nd); *thinks* (nk); *desk* (sk); *spell* (sp)

Other: *clinic* (2 closed syllables)

Sight Words & High-Frequency Words

a, am, an, at, have, he, her, his, I, is, of, says, see, she, that, the, this, to, up, wants, what, works, you, your

Challenge Words & Phrases

appointment, doctor, first name, Hill Street Clinic, last name

expression: *I am sick of _____.*

GRAMMAR & LANGUAGE STRUCTURES

- *then* (with time, e.g., *Then Pam stands up.*)
- *what* questions
- *your, his* (possessive pronouns)

LIFE SKILLS

- dialogues at the front desk of a clinic, hospital, or doctor's office
- languages used at a clinic, translators
- stating and spelling your name aloud
- waiting rooms

A Bad Cold

TARGET VOCABULARY

Word Analysis

Short vowels/CVC: *bad, can, can't; bed, get, tells, well; fix, Hill, ill, pills, will; Bob, lot; but*

Consonant digraphs: *things, with* (th)

Consonant blends: *drink* (dr); *help* (lp); *asks* (sk); *rest* (st)

Other: *clinic, upset* (2 closed syllables)

Sight Words & High-Frequency Words

a, don't, go, have, he, home, I, in, is, my, need, the, to, says, some, work, you

Challenge Words & Phrases

cold, doctor, go home, Hill Street Clinic, water

wellness: *get well, I don't feel well*

GRAMMAR & LANGUAGE STRUCTURES

- *a lot of*
- *can* vs. *can't*
- *can't, don't* (contractions)
- *go home, get rest, drink water* (imperatives in doctor's orders)
- *will* (to denote future)

LIFE SKILLS

- **colds:** prevention and remedies, home or alternative remedies
- talking with a doctor, understanding a doctor's advice
- what happens at a doctor's appointment

The Doctor Costs a Lot

TARGET VOCABULARY

Word Analysis

Short vowels/CVC: *can, Pam; get, tell, yes; bill, Hill, him, sits, will; Bob, lot, not*

Consonant digraphs: *much* (ch); *thank, think, with* (th)

Consonant blends: *help* (lp); *thank, think* (nk); *plans* (pl); *asks, desk* (sk); *costs, stops* (st)

Sight Words & High-Frequency Words

a, about, at, do, does, don't, for, go, has, have, he, home, I, if, is, it, of, says, she, sees, some, that, the, to, too, you

Challenge Words & Phrases

doctor, happy, health plan/s, Hill Street Clinic, maybe, ready

money: *cost a lot, costs too much, $75.00*

GRAMMAR & LANGUAGE STRUCTURES

- *about* (preposition, e.g., *tell about, think about*)
- *do, does, don't*
- *maybe*
- *too much, a lot* (money quantifiers)
- *will* (to denote future)

LIFE SKILLS

- cost of/paying for health care
- low-cost health plans (e.g., state-run health care plans)
- Who can help with health care plans?

Get Rid of Stress

TARGET VOCABULARY

Word Analysis

Short vowels/CVC: *can; get, well; Hill, kids, Kim, quit, rid, will, win; jobs, lot/s, not; but, fun*

Consonant digraphs: *much* (ch); *that, then, think/s, with* (th)

Consonant blends: *help/s* (lp); *and* (nd); *thinks* (nk); *rest* (st); *stress* (str)

Sight Words & High-Frequency Words

at, do, don't, good, has, have, I, is, my, need, of, or, problem, says, she, some, the, to, too, two, what, work, you

Challenge Words & Phrases

doctor, eat, food, get rid of, good, Hill Street Clinic, money, time, too much

exercise: *exercise, jog, walk*

GRAMMAR & LANGUAGE STRUCTURES

- *but* (to signal change of direction)
- *do* vs. *don't*
- *too much* (quantifier)
- *will* (to denote future)

LIFE SKILLS

- doctor's advice, talking to a doctor
- exercise
- healthy foods, healthy living
- stress and its effects, ways to manage stress

Kim's Plan

TARGET VOCABULARY

Word Analysis

Short vowels/CVC: *can, plan; bed, get, tells; kids, Kim, quit, rid; lot; but, fun*

Consonant digraphs: *much* (ch); *then, think/s, with* (th)

Consonant blends: *and* (nd); *rest* (st); *stress* (str)

Other: *park* (r-controlled vowel)

Sight Words & High-Frequency Words

a, at, be, go, good, have, help/s, her, home, I, is, me, more, my, of, says, to, want, we, you

Challenge Words & Phrases

eat, food, get rid of, go to bed, good, together, too much

health: *eat good food, exercise, feel better, go to bed early, healthy, rest, walk*

GRAMMAR & LANGUAGE STRUCTURES

- *can*
- *have to* vs. *want to*
- *too much/a lot*
- *will* (to denote future)

LIFE SKILLS

- exercise
- healthy behaviors
- managing stress

Lesson Notes—Long Vowels

Welcome to Hill Street

TARGET VOCABULARY

Word Analysis

Long-vowel digraphs: *street* (ee)

Final *e* rule: *James, name; these; Home*

Other: *husband* (2 closed syllables)

Sight Words & High-Frequency Words

a, an, are, at, has, her, hey, in, is, on, the, this, to, with

Challenge Words & Phrases

apartment, block, busy, friends, here, husband, lives, welcome

address: *24 Hill Street*

GRAMMAR & LANGUAGE STRUCTURES

- *here is* (in introductions)
- *lives at, lives there*
- *'s* (with possessives)
- *this is* vs. *these are*

LIFE SKILLS

- describing a street block
- personal introductions (*Here is . . .*)

Family

A Letter from School

TARGET VOCABULARY

Word Analysis

Long-vowel digraphs: *Dean, please, speak, teacher* (ea); *meeting, need, see, week* (ee)

Final *e* rule: *home, hope*

Other: *letter, teacher* (-*er* ending); *meeting* (-*ing* ending)

Sight Words & High-Frequency Words

a, about, and, are, asks, be, from, go, her, I, is, my, says, the, this, to, we, what, you

Challenge Words & Phrases

dear, gives, here, letter, school

meetings: *The meeting will be on Monday/at 7:00 p.m./at the school.*

letters: *Dear parent:; From, Miss Dean*

GRAMMAR & LANGUAGE STRUCTURES

- *her, my* (possessive pronouns)
- *need* vs. *need to*
- *please* (in requests)
- *will* (to denote future)

LIFE SKILLS

- looking for details, e.g., date, time, place
- parents' involvement in schools, parent-teacher meetings

- reading and replying to letters from school
- reading and writing letters

A Day with the Kids

TARGET VOCABULARY

Word Analysis

Long-vowel digraphs: *Gail, rain/s, train, wait* (ai); *away, day, Jay's, May, play/s, Saturday, today* (ay)

Other: *pair* (-*air* family); *daughter, soccer* (-*er* ending)

Sight Words & High-Frequency Words

a, are, at, can't, for, from, get, go, has, have, her, is, says, she, the, they, to, too, we

Challenge Words & Phrases

daughter, every, Jay's Pizza, lunch, park, play soccer, soccer, starts, still, watch

expressions: *get away from, go for lunch, have fun*

days & times: *every Saturday, morning, 11:30 a.m.*

GRAMMAR & LANGUAGE STRUCTURES

- *can* vs. *can't*
- *every* (quantifier)
- *let's* (imperative)
- *must*
- *too*

LIFE SKILLS

- children's activities; organized sports for kids
- meeting friends through children
- regular weekend activities
- spending time with children

Pam Needs Day Care

TARGET VOCABULARY

Word Analysis

Long-vowel digraphs: *Main* (ai); *day, maybe, Play* (ay); *need/s, Street* (ee)

Final *e* rule: *James, names, place, rates, safe, Space, take/s; time; home*

Other: *husband, until* (2 closed syllables)

Sight Words & High-Frequency Words

a, about, at, can, for, from, get, go, good, has, help, her, is, it, of, on, she, the, to, too, wants, who, with, work/s, you

Challenge Words & Phrases

baby, friends, husband, make a trip, or, problem

day care: *good place, good rates, names, Play Space, safe, take care of*

times: *9:00 a.m., 1:00 p.m., 1:30 p.m., 2:00 p.m., 5:00 p.m.*

work: from 9:00 a.m. to 1:00/5:00 p.m., full-time, part-time

GRAMMAR & LANGUAGE STRUCTURES

- *but* (to signal change of direction)
- *from* and *to* (with time periods)
- *has* vs. *has to*
- *too*
- *who* questions
- *will* (to denote future)

LIFE SKILLS

- child-care options/things to look for in a good child-care provider
- part-time vs. full-time jobs
- sharing child-care responsibility with family members

A Place for the Kids to Play

TARGET VOCABULARY

Word Analysis

Long-vowel digraphs: *maybe, play* (ay); *clean* (ea); *need, street* (ee)

Final *e* rule: *games, gate, James, make, place, rake, safe, space*

Other: *all* (*-all* family); *husband, tenants* (2 closed syllables)

Sight Words & High-Frequency Words

a, are, for, good, he, help, her, in, is, it, not, of, on, put, says, she, some, the, their, there, they, to, we, with

Challenge Words & Phrases

behind, fix, know, landlord, mess, steps, tenants, thinks, watch

yard: *big space, fix, good place/not a good place for kids, plant grass, put up gate, rocks, safe/not safe, sticks, trash*

GRAMMAR & LANGUAGE STRUCTURES

- adjectives (e.g., *big space, safe place*)
- *but* (to signal change of direction)
- *can*
- *it is* vs. *it is not*
- *put up*
- *there is* vs. *there are*
- *will* (to denote future)

LIFE SKILLS

- places for kids to play
- tenants working together
- yard work, clean up

Parents' Night at the School

TARGET VOCABULARY

Word Analysis

Long-vowel digraphs: *Monday* (ay); *teacher/s* (ea); *need, week* (ee)

Final *e* rule: *crime, knife, knives, Price, time*

Other: *fight/s, night, tonight* (*-ight*); *clinic, teacher* (2 closed syllables)

Sight Words & High-Frequency Words

a, about, and, are, ask, at, can, do, don't, for, go, got, had, he, is, of, on, our, says, talk, the, they, to, want, we, what, with, you

Challenge Words & Phrases

a lot of, boy, into, lunch, or, parents, Parents' Night, school, teacher/s, watch
question: *What do you think . . . ?*

GRAMMAR & LANGUAGE STRUCTURES

- *can*
- *cut, got into, had, had to* (past tense)
- *have* vs. *have to*
- *want* vs. *don't want* (negatives)

LIFE SKILLS

- crime, fights, and violence in schools
- parents & teachers working together
- parents' involvement in schools
- police and their presence at schools

A Parent's Ideas about Crime

TARGET VOCABULARY

Word Analysis

Long-vowel digraphs: *teach, teacher/s* (ea)
Final *e* rule: *same; advice, crime, fine, like, Price, side, smiles; more*
Other: *night, right* (-ight); *parent/s, teacher/s* (2 closed syllables)

Sight Words & High-Frequency Words

a, about, , are, ask, at, can, do, for, have, it, is, our, says, school, tells, talk, the, there, we, what, with, work

Challenge Words & Phrases

all, clap hands, cops, give, have a problem, ideas, just, plan, right, same side, side by side, stands up, teach, think, wrong
question: *What do you think . . . ?*

GRAMMAR & LANGUAGE STRUCTURES

- *but* (to signal change of direction)
- *have to*
- *there is*
- *will* (to denote future)
- *work with*

LIFE SKILLS

- making/presenting a plan
- right and wrong
- taking sides, being on the same side
- working together

Ben Helps a Friend

TARGET VOCABULARY

Word Analysis

Long-vowel digraphs: *maybe, Monday, today* (ay)
Final *e* rule: *alone, close, home, hope, smokes, stole, store*

Sight Words & High-Frequency Words

a, asks, at, be, can, can't, do, don't, from, good, got, has, he, his, I, in, is,
it, my, on, says, talk, the, to, too, want/s, with, work, you

Challenge Words & Phrases

a lot, bad stuff, desk, do drugs, friend, maybe, Monday, park, problem, proud, six-pack,
skips class, soda, upset

Expressions: *I think . . . , I don't think so., What's the matter?*

Drugs-related: *do drugs, got drugs*

GRAMMAR & LANGUAGE STRUCTURES

- *do* vs. *don't*
- *got, stole* (past tense)

LIFE SKILLS

- helping friends who have problems
- kids and drugs

Home

Can the Landlord Raise the Rent?

TARGET VOCABULARY

Word Analysis

Long-vowel digraphs: *mail, raise,* (ai); *May, pay, today* (ay); *keep* (ee)

Other: *fair, repairs (-air* family); *after, letter (-er* ending)

Sight Words & High-Frequency Words

a, for, from, go, got, have, he, in, is, it, not, of, the, this, to, wants, we, with, you

Challenge Words & Phrases

apartment, as of, happy, keep up with costs, landlord, must, pay for repairs, rent, tenant

rent: *raise the rent, rent will go up, $550 a month for rent*

dates: *every year, as of May 1, after 2 months, March, May*

letters: *Dear tenant:, From, Gus, the Landlord*

GRAMMAR & LANGUAGE STRUCTURES

- *can* questions
- *every* (as a time qualifier, e.g., *every year*)
- *have to* and *must* (to show necessity)
- *will* (to denote future)

LIFE SKILLS

- letters from the landlord
- months of the year time lines
- rent increases
- writing/reading letters

Help with the Lease

TARGET VOCABULARY

Word Analysis

Long-vowel digraphs: *raise* (ai); *pay* (ay); *increase, lease, mean, read/s,*
speak/s (ea); *keep, need, see* (ee)

Other: *after, letter (-er* ending)

Sight Words & High-Frequency Words

a, about, and, ask, be, can, can't, for, from, gets, go, got, has, he, help, his, I, is, says, tells, the, to, was, what, with, your

Challenge Words & Phrases

landlord, year

expressions: *I am sorry, I didn't mean to . . .*

rent: *rent increase, increase the rent, raise the rent, keep the rent at $450, rent will be $450*

dates: *for 1 year, after 1 year*

GRAMMAR & LANGUAGE STRUCTURES

- *can* vs. *can't*
- *got* vs. *get* (past vs. present)
- *his landlord, Gus* (appositives)
- *will* (to denote future)

LIFE SKILLS

- dealing with tenant/landlord issues
- getting help from friends
- leases and reading a lease
- making apologies
- rent increases

Junk Mail

TARGET VOCABULARY

Word Analysis

Long-vowel digraphs: *mail* (ai); *today* (ay); *teach* (ea); *sees, week* (ee)

Final *e* rule: *like; home*

Other: *letter* (-er), *mailbox* (2 closed syllables)

Sight Words & High-Frequency Words

a, at, do, from, how, in, it, looks, says, she, the, they, this, to, want, we, what, work, you, your

Challenge Words & Phrases

back from work, fast, get rich, gets home from work, how to get rich, just, looks like, open/s, teach, walks in, watch it

mail: *Dear Friend, Get rich!, get the mail, junk mail, mailbox, Open quick!, opens the letter, send us*

money: *$50, $5000*

GRAMMAR & LANGUAGE STRUCTURES

- *do* questions (e.g., *Do you want . . . ? What do you think?*)
- *Open quick!, Get rich!, Send us $50 today., Watch it.* (imperatives)

LIFE SKILLS

- asking advice from others
- get-rich-quick schemes
- types of mail, including junk mail & advertisements

A Clean-Up Date

TARGET VOCABULARY

Word Analysis

Long-vowel digraphs: *rain* (ai); *Friday* (ay); *clean* (ea); *meet, meeting, street* (ee)

Final *e* rule: *basement, date, James, make, place, safe, take*

Other: *stairs* (-*air* family); *landlord, tenants* (2 closed syllables)

Sight Words & High-Frequency Words

a, are, have, he, help, is, it, of, on, she, the, they, to, too, we

Challenge Words & Phrases

basement, boxes, clean up, every month, fix up the place, get rid of, landlord, last month, make plans, our, problem, set a date, set up a pump, tenants

GRAMMAR & LANGUAGE STRUCTURES

- *can*
- *every* (as a time qualifier, e.g., *every month*)
- *let's* (imperative)
- *to be* (in descriptions: *boxes are wet, stairs are not safe*)
- *will* (to denote future)

LIFE SKILLS

- describing problems in a house/apartment
- flooding in a basement
- working together to solve problems in an apartment building (tenants' meetings)

Jack Smells Smoke

TARGET VOCABULARY

Word Analysis

Long-vowel digraphs: *need, Street* (ee)

Final *e* rule: *alone, close, home, phone, smoke*

Other: *calls, hall* (-*all* family)

Sight Words & High-Frequency Words

are, from, he, help, his, is, there, this, we, where, you

Challenge Words & Phrases

apartment, door, hello, knocks, no one, not a good smell, on the way, smells smoke, something

addresses: *Apartment 6, 24 Hill Street*

emergencies: *911, We need help!*

questions: *Where are you? Where is the smoke?*

GRAMMAR & LANGUAGE STRUCTURES

- *there is*
- *where* questions

LIFE SKILLS

- calling 911, describing an emergency
- emergency situations
- fires in the house
- giving your address

A Fire Truck Stops at Hill Street

TARGET VOCABULARY

Word Analysis
Long-vowel digraphs: *Street* (ee)
Final *e* rule: *fire, fireman/firemen; home, hose, phone, smoke, stove*
Other: *kitchen* (2 closed syllables)

Sight Words & High-Frequency Words
a, at, don't, from, go, have, he, I, is, of, on, talk, the, there, they, to, up, you, your

Challenge Words & Phrases
a lot of, Apartment 6, check the stove, get off the truck, landlord, no one, on the stove, problem, set up, smash in the door, smelled, turn off
fires: *fire truck, fireman/firemen, set up the hose, smoke alarm(s), smoke alarm go off*

GRAMMAR & LANGUAGE STRUCTURES
- *but* (to signal change of direction)
- *-ed* ending (with past tense, e.g., *smelled*)
- *must* (to show necessity)
- *there is*

LIFE SKILLS
- firefighters and their equipment (*hose, helmet, mask, coat, etc.*)
- fires in the home; How do fires start?
- smoke alarms in the apartment/house

Stop Crime on Our Block

TARGET VOCABULARY

Word Analysis
Long-vowel digraphs: *Friday, maybe* (ay); *speak* (ea); *see/s, Street* (ee)
Final *e* rule: *saves, takes; Steve; crime, life, like, Pine, time, vice, wine; Jones*
Other: *call/s* (-all); *tonight* (-ight)

Sight Words & High-Frequency Words
a, about, for, get, he, help, I, in, into, is, it, on, our, says, sees, she, tells, the, there, they, this, to, want/s, we, will

Challenge Words & Phrases
cop, lives, man/woman, meeting, near, on our block, rob the shop, stands up, story, tenants
crimes: *Block Watch, call the cops if we see a crime, help stop crime, watch for crime*
time & day: *7:00 p.m. on Friday*

GRAMMAR & LANGUAGE STRUCTURES
- *can*
- *-s* ending (with present tense, e.g., *calls, helps, saves,* etc.)
- *there is*
- *wants to*
- *will* (to denote future)

- crimes in the neighborhood
- neighborhood watch programs
- talking with police
- tenants' meetings
- ways to deal with crime

Shopping

A Good Deal on Fans

TARGET VOCABULARY

Word Analysis

Long-vowel digraphs: *today* (ay); *beat, deal, heat* (ea); *breeze, feels, feet, free, green, keep, need, see/s, sleep* (ee)

Final *e* rule: *rides; home, Store*

Other: *sign* (-*ign*)

Sight Words & High-Frequency Words

a, asks, can, can't, do, for, get, have, he, his, I, in, is, it, on, put/s, says, that, the, this, to, too, we, with, works, you

Challenge Words & Phrases

buys, cook, cool, goes, good, now, puts up his feet, sets up, very, vest

shopping: *buy/s, buy 1, get 1 free, Do you have . . . ?, get a good deal, Home Store, man in a green vest*

heat: *beat the heat, feel the breeze, keep cool, too hot*

numbers: *1, 2*

GRAMMAR & LANGUAGE STRUCTURES

- *beat the heat, get a good deal, buy 1, get 1 free* (imperatives)
- *it is . . .* (to describe weather)
- numerals vs. number words (*1* vs. *one*)
- *-s* ending (with present tense, e.g., *asks, buys, feels,* etc.)
- *to* vs. *too*

LIFE SKILLS

- asking for help in a store
- dealing with heat
- describing weather conditions
- signs in stores
- types of sales, e.g., buy 1, get 1 free

A Meal at Burger Hut

TARGET VOCABULARY

Word Analysis

Long-vowel digraphs: *may, pays* (ay); *cream, eat/s, Jean, meal, please, seats, speaks, teas, treat* (ea); *cheeseburger, green* (ee)

Other: *salad* (2 closed syllables)

Sight Words & High-Frequency Words

a, about, are, at, can, go, good, have, help, her, how, I, is, it, let's, on, she, that, the, they, wants, with

Challenge Words & Phrases

at the end of, Friday, How about . . . ?, treat

fast food: *Burger Hut, cashier, go and get seats, May I help you?, picks up the food, please, That will be . . .*

food: *cheeseburger, green salad, ice cream, iced tea(s), meal*

time & day: *8:00 p.m. on Friday*

GRAMMAR & LANGUAGE STRUCTURES

• *may* questions (*May I help you?*)

• *her* (possessive pronoun)

• *please* in polite requests

LIFE SKILLS

• names of food items

• ordering food at restaurants

• types of restaurants (e.g., fast food)

A Rain Check on Paint

TARGET VOCABULARY

Word Analysis

Long-vowel digraphs: *paint, rain, wait* (ai); *days, gray, today* (ay); *see* (ee)

Final *e* rule: *sale; home, store*

Other: *call* (-*all* family); *kitchen* (2 closed syllables)

Sight Words & High-Frequency Words

a, am, are, asks, at, can, comes, do, for, get, go, has, have, he, his, I, in, is, it, more, of, on, says, some, tells, the, then, to, wants, we, what, when, where, you

Challenge Words & Phrases

bring in, comes back, goes to, I am sorry.

shopping: *buy paint, clerk, go and see, Home Store, more paint on the way, out of gray paint, rain check, sale price, wait here*

time: *3 or 4 days*

GRAMMAR & LANGUAGE STRUCTURES

• *but* (to signal change of direction)

• *has* vs. *has to*

• *or* (to signal alternatives)

• *what* and *where* questions

• *will* (to denote future)

LIFE SKILLS

• asking for help, talking to store clerks

• buying things on sale

• colors

• rain checks

A Birthday Gift for Liz

TARGET VOCABULARY

Word Analysis

Long-vowel digraphs: *chain, plain* (ai); *birthday, day(s), layaway, pay, today* (ay); *fee, sees* (ee)

Final *e* rule: *use*
Other: *mall* (-all); *gold, hold* (-old)

Sight Words & High-Frequency Words

a, about, asks, at, can, can't, come, don't, for, get, go, good, has, have, her,
how, I, in, is, it, looks, put, says, she, the, this, to, want/s, we, with, you

Challenge Words & Phrases

bank, birthday, cash, clerk, gift, How much is . . . ?, looks at, pay for
days: *Tuesday, 30 days, for 1 day*
layaway: *put on layaway, $5 fee, hold for 30 days, come back and pay the rest*
money: *$5, $10, $15, $25*

GRAMMAR & LANGUAGE STRUCTURES

- *can*
- *doesn't/don't want to*
- *has to (get)*
- *pay* and *come back* (imperatives, e.g., *Pay $10 today., Come back and pay the rest.*)
- questions with *how much*
- *to be* (verb)
- *will* (to denote future)

LIFE SKILLS

- birthdays
- buying on layaway, store layaway policies
- fees

How Can I Save?

TARGET VOCABULARY

Word Analysis

Long-vowel digraphs: *day, pays, way* (ay); *each* (ea); *needs, see* (ee)
Final *e* rule: *bake, plane, sale, save/s, take, wage(s); time; home, more*

Sight Words & High-Frequency Words

a, at, can, does, don't, for, gets, good, has, have, he, his, how, I, it, looks, not,
of, on, puts, the, then, to, wants, will, work

Challenge Words & Phrases

bank, bills, buy things, cook, family, good wage, left after, plane fare, take a
trip, $20 left, walk to work, ways to save
time: *a long time, a month, after, each month, every day*

GRAMMAR & LANGUAGE STRUCTURES

- *after, each month, every day, next month, then* (time qualifiers)
- *but* (to signal change of direction)
- *can*
- *want/s to*

LIFE SKILLS

- bank accounts
- paying bills and budgeting
- reasons for saving money, e.g., visiting the family
- wages: weekly, biweekly, or monthly
- ways to save money (formal and informal)

Check the Size!

TARGET VOCABULARY

Word Analysis

Long-vowel digraphs: *Monday, Wednesday* (ay)

Final *e* rule: *line, nice, price, size, time; store*

Other: *right, tight* (-ight); *jacket* (2 closed syllables)

Sight Words & High-Frequency Words

a, at, did, for, go, good, got, had, has, have, he, I, is, not, the, this, to, too, want, was, what, work, you, your

Challenge Words & Phrases

another, jacket, men's store, Monday, much, try on, Wednesday

size: *check the size, fit/s, right/wrong size, size 36, size 38, too tight*

GRAMMAR & LANGUAGE STRUCTURES

- *but* (to signal change of direction)
- *to be* (verb: in descriptions, e.g., *It is tight.*)
- *to* vs. *too*
- *was* vs. *is*, *got* vs. *get* (past tense vs. present tense)
- *what* questions

LIFE SKILLS

- buying things on sale
- clothing sizes, Do you know your sizes?
- describing how clothes fit

The Right Size

TARGET VOCABULARY

Word Analysis

Long-vowel digraphs: *Monday, Wednesday* (ay)

Final *e* rule: *exchange; line, nice, size*

Other: *right, tight* (-ight); *jacket* (2 closed syllables)

Sight Words & High-Frequency Words

a, at, can, can't, for, gets, got, he, helps, I, in, is, on, says, tells, the, with, your

Challenge Words & Phrases

cash back, cashier, clerk, exchange, finds, gets in line, jacket, men's store, next time, return/s

size: *check the size, fit/s, right/wrong size, size 36, size 38, too tight*

GRAMMAR & LANGUAGE STRUCTURES

- *but* (to signal change of direction)
- *May I* questions
- *got* vs. *get* (past tense vs. present tense)

LIFE SKILLS

- exchange vs. return
- getting help in a store
- returning items to stores, return policies

Health

Heart Disease

TARGET VOCABULARY

Word Analysis

Long-vowel digraphs: *today* (ay); *disease, eat, Jean* (ea); *feel, see* (ee)

Final *e* rule: *home, phone*

Other: *better, doctor, upset* (2 closed syllables)

Sight Words & High-Frequency Words

a, about, at, be, can, did, do, do not, for, had, have, help, I, is, my, says, some, talk, tells, the, with, you, your

Challenge Words & Phrases

a lot of people, talk about

health-related: *eat better, feel bad, feel sick, good food, heart, heart disease, my problem, tests*

GRAMMAR & LANGUAGE STRUCTURES

- *but* (to signal change of direction)
- *can*
- *do* and *don't*
- *I* (in describing personal states, e.g., *I feel bad, I don't feel sick, I am upset, I feel better*)
- *'s* (with possessives, e.g., *Pam's mom*)

LIFE SKILLS

- dealing with chronic health problems, e.g., heart disease
- healthy eating, the food pyramid, nutrition
- talking about health problems with doctors, friends, family

Food for the Heart

TARGET VOCABULARY

Word Analysis

Long-vowel digraphs: *beans, disease, eat, grease, Jean, lean, meal, meat* (ea); *feel, green, need, sweets, weekend* (ee)

Other: *dinner, salad, upset* (2 closed syllables)

Sight Words & High-Frequency Words

a, about, can, do, don't, for, good, have, help, her, I, it, let's, my, of, on, says, some, talk, the, to, today, too, we, with, you, your

Challenge Words & Phrases

better, cut out, That's it!

days: *Friday, Sunday*

food: *beans, cook, dinner, fish, good food, grease, green salads, meat, salt, sweets*

health: *feel a lot better, heart disease*

GRAMMAR & LANGUAGE STRUCTURES

- *don't*
- *I* (in describing personal states, e.g., *I am upset, I feel better*)
- *'s* (with possessives)

- dealing with chronic health problems, healthy eating, the food pyramid, nutrition
- talking about health problems with doctors, friends, family

What Does the Health Plan Pay?

TARGET VOCABULARY

Word Analysis

Long-vowel digraphs: *Aid* (ai); *co-pay, days, may, pay, stay* (ay); *see* (ee)

Final *e* rule: *phones*

Other: *clinic, packet, questions* (2 closed syllables); *hospital* (3 closed syllables)

Sight Words & High-Frequency Words

a, about, ask, at, can, for, he, I, is, do, does, get, good, has, have, him, in, of, more, some, tell, the, there, to, up, want/s, we, what, will, you

Challenge Words & Phrases

doctor, got news, Health-Aid, health care plan, hello, hospital, just, most, packet, questions, up to 30 days

money: *$5 co-pay*

GRAMMAR & LANGUAGE STRUCTURES

- *but* (to signal change of direction)
- *do* questions
- *if* questions
- *just, more, most, up to* (time and amount qualifiers)
- *may* (to show possibility)
- *will* (to denote future)

LIFE SKILLS

- asking questions to find out what health care plans cover
- calling a health insurance company
- different kinds of health care plans

Fill in the Form

TARGET VOCABULARY

Word Analysis

Long-vowel digraphs: *Aid, mail* (ai); *pay* (ay)

Final *e* rule: *age, make, name, rate, space, takes, wage; hope*

Other: *care, Clare* (-are), *packet* (2 closed syllables)

Sight Words & High-Frequency Words

a, can, from, gets, good, has, have, help/s, I, in, is, looks, says, she, tells, the, they, to, want/s, we, with, work, you, your

Challenge Words & Phrases

every, fill in, form/s, friend, Health-Aid, health care plan, how much, look at, monthly rate, now, packet

forms: *address, age, monthly wage, name, space*

GRAMMAR & LANGUAGE STRUCTURES

- *fill in*
- *will* (to denote future)
- *you have to* (imperative)
- *your* (possessive pronoun)

- applying for health care
- filling out forms, filling in the spaces on forms
- monthly rates
- types of health care options (state-run, free-care, HMOs, private, etc.)

Exercise Is Good for You

TARGET VOCABULARY

Word Analysis

Long-vowel digraphs: *Jean* (ea); *feel, need, see* (ee)

Final *e* rule: *bike, drive, exercise, fine, miles, nice, ride, smile/s, sometimes, surprise; home*

Sight Words & High-Frequency Words

a, at, did, didn't, do, does, for, get, go, good, has, help, how, I, is, it, my, on, says, tells, the, this, to, was, you

Challenge Words & Phrases

doctor, door, doorbell, exercise, hi, How do you feel?, long, no, now

exercise: *go for a swim, long ride, ride my bike, stretch, 10 miles, walk*

GRAMMAR & LANGUAGE STRUCTURES

- appositives (*Pam's mom, Jean*)
- *had, was* (past tense)
- *I* (in describing personal states, e.g., *I feel . . .*)
- *now, sometimes* (time qualifiers)

LIFE SKILLS

- exercising for one's health
- greeting someone (*Hi. How do you feel? I feel fine.*)
- transportation options
- ways to get exercise

Home from School

TARGET VOCABULARY

Word Analysis

Long-vowel digraphs: *stay/s, today* (ay); *speak* (ea); *feels, Lee, need/s* (ee); *throat* (oa)

Final *e* rule: *take; home, hope, nose, note, phones, robe, sore, woke*

Other: *call* (-all); *better, teacher* (2 closed syllables)

Sight Words & High-Frequency Words

a, at, be, can, does, don't, for, have, her, I, in, is, it, my, says, she, tells, the, this, to, up, we, when, with, you

Challenge Words & Phrases

checks, daughter, hello, just, phones the school, returns to school, send a note, stay/s home, still, teacher, Wednesday, woke up

sickness: *bad cold, don't feel well, feel hot, runny nose, sore throat*

GRAMMAR & LANGUAGE STRUCTURES

- *need to*
- *send* (imperative, e.g., *send a note*)
- *to feel* (verb: to describe sickness, e.g., *I feel hot.*)

- *to have* (verb: to describe sickness, e.g., *I have a bad cold.*)
- *when* (to connect phrases in a sentence)

LIFE SKILLS

- calling the school about a child's absence
- caring for sick children and family members
- colds and how to care for them
- types of illnesses and symptoms of illness

A Note for the Teacher

TARGET VOCABULARY

Word Analysis

Long-vowel digraphs: *day, stay, today* (ay); *Dean, please* (ea); *feel/s, Lee* (ee); *coat, throat* (oa)

Final *e* rule: *write/s; clothes, home, hope, more, nose, note, sore*

Other: *backpack, better, teacher* (2 closed syllables)

Sight Words & High-Frequency Words

a, can, does, don't, for, from, get/s, go, good, had, have, her, I, not, on, put/s, says, she, the, to, too, up, was, will, you, your

Challenge Words & Phrases

give, school, sick, teacher

days: *Wednesday, Thursday*

sickness: *bad cold, feel/s better, runny nose, sore throat*

notes: *write a note; From, Kim Lee*

GRAMMAR & LANGUAGE STRUCTURES

- *get* and *put* (imperatives)
- *had* vs. *have* (past vs. present tense)
- *had to*

LIFE SKILLS

- children's sickness/absence from school
- describing symptoms of illness
- how to excuse a child's absence from school
- writing notes to the teacher

ANSWER KEY

■

Short Vowels: Family

p. 7
1. no
2. yes
3. no
4. yes
5. yes
6. yes
7. no
8. yes
9. yes
10. no

p. 8
1. Jack
2. Bob
3. Pam
4. Kim

p. 12
1. This
2. mother
3. two
4. son
5. daughter
6. kids
7. family
8. They

p. 13
1. is
2. is
3. is
4. are
5. is
6. are

p. 16
1. Kim's kids are Ben and Liz.
2. Liz and Ben go to Hill Top School.
3. It is Monday.
4. The kids get the bus at 7:30 a.m.
5. Kim tells the kids to get their backpacks.
6. Kim and the kids run to the bus stop.

p. 17
1. bus
2. backpack
3. bus stop
4. Liz
5. Ben
6. kids

p. 18
1. It is 7:15.
2. It is not 7:20.
3. It is not 7:30.
4. It is 3:45.
5. It is not 9:00.

p. 21
1. no
2. yes
3. no
4. no
5. no
6. yes
7. no
8. yes
9. yes
10. yes

p. 22
1. study
2. desk
3. good
4. talks
5. sad
6. can
7. help
8. teacher

p. 23
1. at
2. at
3. on
4. at
5. to
6. at
7. to

p. 26
1. Ben (Kim's son) needs help with math.
2. Kim can ask the teacher for help.
3. Kim calls Hill Top School.
4. Miss Pitt is in class.
5. Kim can call back at 4:00 p.m.
6. Kim calls the school on Wednesday and Thursday.

p. 27
1. Tuesday
2. Thursday
3. Saturday, Sunday
4. Wednesday
5. Friday
6. Sunday
7. Saturday
8. Monday

p. 28
1. son
2. needs
3. Miss
4. calls
5. mom
6. class
7. back
8. Thank
9. Tuesday
10. help

p. 31
1. no
2. yes
3. yes
4. yes
5. no
6. no
7. yes
8. yes
9. no
10. yes

p. 32
1. yes
2. no
3. no
4. yes
5. yes
6. no

p. 33
1. is
2. are
3. is
4. are
5. are
6. is

p. 36
1. It is Sunday.
2. It is the weekend.
3. Liz and Ben are watching TV.
4. Kim wants to go to the park.
5. Ben wants to watch TV.
6. Liz wants to run and kick the ball.

p. 37
1. TV
2. home
3. park
4. run
5. school
6. ball

p. 41
1. Kim is at home.
2. She has to mop and dust. She has to wash the pans and the cups. She has to fix dinner.
3. Kim is tired.
4. Ben and Liz help Kim.

p. 42
1. wash cups
2. wash pans
3. mop
4. dust

p. 43
1. do
2. fix
3. wash
4. is
5. dust
6. has

Short Vowels: Home

p. 7
1. This is Hill Street.
2. The clinic is on Hill Street.
3. Jack lives on Hill Street.
4. The kids live with Kim.
5. Pam, Jack, and Kim and the kids live on Hill Street.
6. Bob has a job on Hill Street.

p. 11
1. Jack is in his new apartment.
2. Jack has four rooms.
3. Bob and Pam will help Jack.
4. Pam tells Jack to stop.
5. Bob and Pam and Jack work all day.
6. They unpack one box at a time.

p. 12
1. kitchen
2. bedroom
3. living room
4. bathroom

p. 13
1. new
2. four
3. help
4. box
5. fast
6. one
7. day
8. unpack

p. 16
1. The pots and pans are in the sink.
2. The tub is in the bathroom.
3. The sink is next to the tub.
4. The lamp is next to the fan.
5. The bed is in the bedroom.
6. The rug is under the bed.

p. 17
1. sink
2. tub
3. fan
4. bed
5. rug
6. lamp

p. 18
1. in
2. in
3. in
4. next to
5. in
6. next to
7. in
8. under

p. 21
1. Jack's address is 24 Hill Street, Apartment 3.
2. Pam's address is 24 Hill Street, Apartment 5.

p. 26
1. no
2. yes
3. no
4. yes
5. no
6. yes
7. yes
8. yes
9. no
10. yes

p. 27
1. tub
2. wet
3. has
4. Gus
5. fix
6. fast
7. bath
8. tub
9. tell
10. the

p. 28
1. The bed is broken.
2. The tub is not leaking.
3. The lamp is broken.
4. The sink is not leaking.
5. The sink is leaking.

p. 31
1. no
2. yes
3. no
4. no
5. yes
6. no
7. no
8. no
9. yes
10. no

p. 32
1. plumber
2. mother
3. father
4. doctor

p. 33
1. is
2. is not
3. is
4. is not
5. is

p. 36
1. Kim is in bed.
2. Kim hears the trash truck.
3. The trash truck is at the end of the street.
4. The kids get the glass and cans.
5. Kim grabs the trash.
6. The trash truck stops next to Kim.

p. 37
1. paper
2. glass
3. cans
4. boxes

ANSWER KEY

■

p. 38
1. in
2. at
3. to
4. in
5. in
6. to
7. next to

p. 41
1. Jack pays rent every month.
2. Jack writes a check.
3. The landlord is Gus.
4. Jack pays rent today.
   or
   Jack pays rent on the first day of the month.
5. Jack calls Pam.
6. Pam and Jack give the checks to Gus.

p. 43

Short Vowels: Shopping

p. 7
1. block
2. shops
3. clinic
4. to
5. lives
6. Kim
7. two
8. job

p. 8
1. is
2. has
3. has
4. is
5. has
6. has

p. 13
1. Pam's day off is Saturday.
2. Pam shops on her day off.
3. Pam shops at Home Store, the mall, Save-a-Lot, and Hill Street Fish Market.
4. Pam has to get a pan, a dress, food, and fish.

p. 16
1. yes
2. yes
3. no
4. yes
5. yes
6. yes
7. no
8. yes
9. no
10. yes

p. 17
1. pan
2. dress
3. store
4. home
5. money
6. Pam

p. 18
1. The pan costs a lot.
2. The pan costs a little.
3. The pot costs a little.
4. The pot costs too much.
5. The pots and pans are cheap.

p. 21
1. no
2. no
3. yes
4. yes
5. no
6. yes
7. no
8. yes
9. no
10. no

p. 22
1. mall
2. dress
3. black
4. belt
5. fit
6. off
7. cashier
8. pays

p. 26
1. Pam is at the bus stop.
2. Pam got a dress at the mall.
3. Pam's new dress is in a bag.
4. The dress has a small rip.
5. The cashier said, "This dress is $10 off. But you can't bring it back."

p. 27
1. Pam
2. dress
3. bag
4. rip
5. cashier

p. 28
1. at
2. next to
3. in
4. at
5. in
6. at
7. in
8. in

p. 31
1. no
2. yes
3. yes
4. no
5. yes
6. yes
7. yes
8. no
9. yes
10. yes

p. 32
1. eggs
2. milk
3. ham
4. bread
5. fish
6. jam

p. 33
1. Pam gets 12 eggs.
2. She has to get a dress.
3. The food is in bags.
4. She writes lists.
5. Pam gets a basket.

p. 36
1. Pam is at the supermarket.
2. She has milk, eggs, and jam in her basket.
3. Pam has $10.00 cash.
4. The milk is $2.60.
5. Pam's bill is $7.10.
6. The cashier gives Pam change.

p. 37
1. store
2. food
3. jam
4. cash
5. cashier
6. eggs
7. milk
8. bill
9. gives
10. change

p. 38
1. is
2. are
3. is
4. are
5. is
6. is

p. 41
1. yes
2. yes
3. no
4. yes
5. no
6. no
7. no
8. no
9. no
10. yes

p. 42
1. open
2. closed
3. open
4. open
5. closed
6. closed

p. 43
1. in
2. to
3. to
4. at
5. on
6. on
7. to
8. on

Short Vowels: Health

p. 7
1. yes
2. yes
3. no
4. yes
5. yes
6. no
7. yes
8. no
9. no
10. no

p. 8
1. Hill
2. shops
3. has
4. lives
5. is
6. kids
7. with
8. Street
9. Bob
10. to

p. 11
1. It is Wednesday.
2. Kim's son has a rash.
3. Kim calls Hill Street Clinic.
4. Her son has to see the doctor.
5. Today, the rash is on his hands and legs.
6. She can bring him to the clinic at 1:00 p.m.

p. 12
1. Wednesday
2. rash
3. doctor
4. Pam

5. Monday
6. Tuesday
7. hands
8. son

p. 13
1. is
2. is
3. has
4. has
5. is
6. is

p. 16
1. yes
2. yes
3. no
4. yes
5. no
6. yes
7. no
8. no
9. yes
10. no

p. 17
1. bed
2. work
3. boss
4. sick
5. well
6. get
7. clinic
8. thanks
9. call
10. today

p. 18
1. in
2. in
3. at
4. to
5. to
6. to
7. at
8. to

p. 21
1. Bob is at Hill Street Clinic.
2. Pam works at Hill Street Clinic.
3. Bob tells Pam he has an appointment with the doctor.
4. Bob spells his last name F-I-N-N.
5. Pam tells Bob to sit.
6. The doctor can see Bob.

p. 22
1. well
2. works
3. big
4. appointment
5. spell
6. tells
7. sits
8. doctor

p. 23
1. no
2. yes
3. no
4. yes
5. no
6. no

p. 26
1. yes
2. no
3. yes
4. no
5. no
6. yes
7. no
8. no
9. yes
10. yes

p. 27
1. with
2. feel
3. cold
4. tells
5. drink
6. asks
7. Pills
8. fix
9. rest
10. will

ANSWER KEY

p. 31
1. no
2. yes
3. no
4. no
5. yes
6. no
7. no
8. no
9. yes
10. yes

p. 32
1. ready
2. bill
3. not
4. too much
5. help
6. plan
7. cost
8. health

p. 33
1. at
2. to
3. at
4. to
5. about
6. about

p. 36
1. Kim is not well.
2. Kim has two jobs.
3. The doctor tells Kim to get lots of rest, eat good food, and exercise.
4. Kim can walk to work.
5. She can exercise with the kids.

p. 37
1. Kim
2. doctor
3. money
4. exercise
5. rest
6. kids

p. 38
1. a little money
2. a lot of money
3. a lot of money
4. a little money
5. a little money

Long Vowels: Family

p. 7
1. Kim
2. Jack
3. Pam
4. Bob

p. 8
1. Jack, Kim, and Pam live at 24 Hill Street.
2. Jack lives in an apartment.
3. Kim lives with her kids.
4. Bob has a job on Hill Street.
5. Pam lives with her husband.
6. Her husband's name is James.

p. 11
1. yes
2. no
3. yes
4. yes
5. no
6. yes
7. yes
8. no
9. yes
10. yes

p. 12
1. letter
2. please
3. parent
4. teacher
5. meeting
6. speak
7. need
8. week

p. 13
1. from
2. to
3. from
4. to
5. at
6. on
7. at
8. to

p. 16
1. yes
2. no
3. yes
4. yes
5. yes
6. yes
7. no
8. yes
9. no
10. yes

p. 17
1. park
2. pair
3. rain
4. train
5. pizza

p. 18
1. is
2. is
3. is
4. are
5. are
6. are
7. are
8. are
9. is
10. is

p. 21
1. no
2. no
3. yes
4. yes
5. yes
6. yes
7. yes
8. no
9. yes
10. yes

p. 22
1. baby
2. care
3. day care
4. take
5. Play Space
6. place
7. safe
8. rates

p. 23
1. It is not 9:00 a.m.
2. It is not 1:30 p.m.
3. It is 5:00.
4. It is 1:30 p.m.
5. It is 2:00 a.m.

p. 26
1. The kids play in the street.
2. The kids need a safe place to play.
3. Pam knows of a big space.
4. The space is behind 24 Hill Street.
5. The landlord will not fix the space.
6. The tenants can make a safe place for the kids.

p. 27
1. grass
2. sticks
3. gate
4. steps
5. rocks
6. rake

p. 28
1. There is some grass.
2. There is a lot of trash.
3. There are some sticks.
4. There is some trash.
5. There are a lot of rocks.

p. 31
1. yes
2. no
3. no
4. yes
5. yes
6. no
7. yes
8. yes
9. yes
10. yes

p. 32
1. cop
2. clinic
3. guns
4. knife
5. knives
6. lunch

p. 33
1. parents
2. teachers
3. teacher
4. parents
5. kids
6. knife
7. fight
8. kid
9. fights
10. knives

p. 36
1. problem
2. plan
3. cops
4. Kim
5. talk
6. kids
7. Parents
8. Mr. Price

p. 37
1. wrong
2. ideas
3. advice
4. clap
5. same
6. right
7. side
8. fine
9. smiles
10. work

p. 38
1. side by side
2. good advice
3. right from wrong
4. same side
5. good advice
6. same side
7. side by side
8. right from wrong

p. 41
1. no
2. yes
3. no
4. yes
5. no
6. no
7. yes
8. no
9. yes
10. yes

p. 42
1. smokes
2. skips
3. stole
4. stuff
5. close
6. proud
7. alone
8. upset

p. 43
1. What's
2. can't
3. don't
4. What's
5. don't

Long Vowels: Home

p. 7
1. yes
2. yes
3. yes
4. yes
5. no
6. no
7. yes
8. yes
9. yes
10. yes

p. 11
1. Jack got a letter today.
2. The letter is from the landlord.
3. Gus is the landlord.
4. Jack is not happy. He thinks it is not fair.
5. Jack got the apartment in March.
6. Gus will raise the rent in May.

p. 12
1. apartment
2. tenant
3. landlord
4. pay
5. repairs
6. rent
7. raise
8. fair

p. 13
Dear Tenant:
We have to raise the rent every year.
We have to pay for repairs.
We have to keep up with costs.
We will raise the rent in May.
As of May 1, you must pay $625 a month for rent.
From,
Pete, the Landlord

p. 16
1. yes
2. no
3. yes
4. yes
5. yes
6. yes
7. no
8. yes
9. no
10. yes

p. 17
1. read
2. speak
3. keep
4. increase
5. needs
6. reads
7. speaks
8. mean
9. keep
10. increase

ANSWER KEY

∎

---

p. 18
1. from
2. to
3. from
4. from
5. for
6. for
7. to
8. from
9. to
10. For

p. 21
1. no
2. yes
3. no
4. no
5. yes
6. no
7. yes
8. no
9. no
10. yes

p. 22
1. mailbox
2. mail
3. junk mail
4. cash
5. trash

p. 23
Dear Friend,
I want to help you.
I will teach you to get rich quick.
Send me $100 today.
You will get $1,000 in a week.

p. 26
1. The tenants meet every month.
   or
   The tenants meet at 7:00 p.m. on Friday.
2. Rain got in the basement.
3. The landlord will fix the stairs.
4. The landlord will set up a pump.
5. The tenants will clean the basement.
6. They will clean the basement on Saturday.

p. 27
1. month
2. week
3. year
4. time
5. date *or* day
6. day
7. month
8. year
9. date
10. time

p. 28
1. The stairs are not safe.
2. The boxes are wet.
3. The basement is clean.
4. The place is not safe.
5. The place is clean.

p. 31
1. Jack is at home.
   or
   Jack is in his apartment on Hill Street.
2. Jack smells smoke.
3. The smoke is from Apartment 6.
4. No one is home in Apartment 6.
5. Jack gets the phone.
6. Jack calls 911.

p. 32
1. smoke
2. hall
3. closed
4. alone
5. phone

p. 33
1. in
2. on
3. smells
4. smell
5. runs
6. gets
7. calls
8. need
9. in
10. on

p. 36
1. no
2. yes
3. yes
4. yes
5. no
6. yes
7. yes
8. no
9. no
10. yes

p. 37
1. fire truck
2. firemen
3. fire hose
4. fire
5. stove
6. smoke alarm

p. 38
1. He
2. I
3. We
4. You
5. We
6. He

p. 41
1. no
2. no
3. yes
4. no
5. yes
6. yes
7. no
8. no
9. yes
10. yes

p. 42
1. story
2. wine shop
3. Pine Street
4. rob
5. Block Watch
6. time
7. crime
8. life

Long Vowels: Shopping

p. 8
1. busy
2. shopping
3. supermarket
4. block
5. apartments
6. kids
7. works
8. Bob

p. 11
1. no
2. yes
3. no
4. no
5. yes
6. yes
7. no
8. yes
9. yes
10. no

p. 12
1. vest
2. fan
3. fans
4. feet
5. breeze

p. 13
1. rides
2. goes
3. Get
4. get
5. gets
6. goes
7. sets up
8. puts up
9. get
10. gets

p. 16
1. Pam and Jean are at Burger Hut.
2. Pam wants a cheeseburger.
3. Jean wants a green salad.
4. Pam pays the cashier.
5. Pam and Jean go and get seats.
6. They have ice cream for a treat.

p. 17
1. green salad
2. cheeseburger
3. ice cream
4. iced tea
5. seat
6. cashier

p. 21
1. yes
2. yes
3. yes
4. yes
5. no
6. yes
7. yes
8. yes
9. yes
10. yes

p. 22
1. paint
2. on sale
3. gray
4. clerk
5. see
6. rain check
7. sale price
8. wait

p. 23
1. wants
2. waits
3. comes
4. says
5. get
6. get
7. call
8. bring
9. pay
10. wait

p. 26
1. The gold chain is for Liz.
2. The chain is $25.
3. Kim has $15.
4. The layaway fee is $5.
5. The clerk can hold the chain for 1 day.
6. Kim will go to the bank.

p. 27
1. mall
2. plain
3. gift
4. birthday
5. layaway
6. fee
7. chain
8. cash

p. 28
1. gift
2. gold
3. cash
4. fee
5. fee
6. free
7. hold
8. hold
9. cash
10. pay

p. 31
1. yes
2. no
3. no
4. yes
5. yes
6. no
7. no
8. yes
9. yes
10. yes

p. 32
1. plane
2. fare
3. wage
4. fair
5. monthly
6. month
7. fare
8. fare
9. sale
10. month

p. 36
1. jacket
2. Monday
3. time
4. try
5. size
6. tight
7. Wednesday
8. another

p. 37
1. nice
2. price
3. try
4. check
5. too
6. tight
7. size
8. time
9. try
10. right

p. 38
1. The jacket is too tight.
2. The hat is the wrong size.
3. It is too tight.
4. The price is not good.
5. The TV is a good price.

p. 41
1. yes
2. no
3. yes
4. yes
5. no
6. yes
7. yes
8. yes
9. yes
10. yes

p. 42
1. cashier
2. fit
3. return
4. exchange
5. find
6. returns
7. line
8. back

p. 43
Sample answer:
This jacket does not fit.
It is the wrong size for me.
It is too tight.
Can I exchange it?
Can I get the right size?

ANSWER KEY

■

Long Vowels: Health

p. 7
1. Jack   4. Pam
2. Kim   5. James
3. Bob

p. 11
1. Jean is Pam's mom.
2. Jean is upset.
3. Jean went to see the doctor.
4. Jean's problem is heart disease.
5. Jean can eat better.
6. Pam and Jean can talk about the things Jean eats.

p. 12
1. heart disease   5. tests
2. sick   6. heart
3. upset   7. better
4. doctor   8. eat

p. 13
1. went   6. had
2. did   7. do
3. had   8. do
4. has   9. have
5. have   10. go

p. 16
1. no   6. yes
2. yes   7. no
3. yes   8. yes
4. yes   9. yes
5. yes   10. yes

p. 17
1. salad   4. meat
2. beans   5. sweets
3. fish   6. salt

p. 21
1. Bob wants to get a health care plan.
2. There is a good plan at the clinic.
3. The name of the plan is Health-Aid.
4. The co-pay is $5.
5. Health-Aid pays for up to 30 days in the hospital.
6. The packet will tell Bob more about the plan.

p. 22
1. Health-Aid   5. doctor
2. health plan   6. co-pay
3. clinic   7. hospital
4. questions   8. packet

p. 23
1. City Health
2. doctor
3. $15
4. 21

p. 26
1. no   6. no
2. yes   7. yes
3. no   8. yes
4. yes   9. yes
5. yes   10. yes

p. 27
1. care   5. age
2. form   6. wage
3. space   7. rate
4. address   8. monthly

p. 31
1. yes   6. no
2. yes   7. yes
3. no   8. yes
4. yes   9. yes
5. no   10. no

p. 32
1. swim   4. stretch
2. walk   5. ring
3. ride   6. drive

p. 36
1. Liz has a sore throat.
2. Liz has a runny nose.
3. Liz needs to stay home.
4. Kim phones the school.
5. Kim will send a note when Liz returns.
6. Liz will take the note to the teacher.

p. 37
1. woke   6. checks
2. robe   7. cold
3. hot   8. phone
4. sore   9. stays
5. nose   10. note

p. 38
1. has   6. have
2. have   7. has
3. have   8. have
4. have   9. have
5. have   10. has

p. 41
1. Liz was sick on Wednesday.
2. On Thursday, Liz feels better.
3. Liz wants to go to school.
4. Kim checks Liz.
5. Kim writes a note to Miss Dean.
6. Miss Dean is Liz's teacher.

p. 42
1. nose   4. coat
2. throat   5. note
3. clothes

p. 43
1. on   6. on
2. at   7. on
3. at   8. to
4. on   9. to
5. to   10. at